THE ART OF
POSITIVE FEELING

by
Swami Jyotirmayananda

© 1997 Swami Jyotirmayananda
All rights reserved.

Yoga Research Foundation
6111 S.W. 74th Avenue
South Miami, Florida 33143
Tel: (305) 666-2006

ISBN 0-934664-48-X

Library of Congress Catalog Card Number 97-061448

PRINTED IN THE UNITED STATES OF AMERICA

THE ART OF
POSITIVE FEELING

Vidya Patel
May God bless you!
Swami Jyotir
Mer 29/98

Dedicated to
the seekers of true happiness
who are intent upon discovering
the amazing nectar of divine feeling
for the promotion of all that is
true, good and beautiful!

PUBLISHER'S NOTE

In human personality, thought and feeling are interrelated like flower and fragrance. If a person lacks profound feeling, his thoughts become weak and ineffective. On the other hand, if his thought is negative and ego-centric, the feelings of his heart become like a polluted stream—tinged with anger, hate, pride and various impurities.

Having written his much acclaimed book, *The Art of Positive Thinking*, Sri Swami Jyotirmayananda felt the need of writing a supplementary book, *The Art of Positive Feeling*. These two books present a complete picture of the mystical art of controlling and culturing the mind for attaining Self-realization.

In this wonderful book, Swami Jyotirmayananda provides a bouquet of colorful stories, joyous humor, and profound insights that will guide you to the unfoldment of sublime feeling within your heart.

The first portion of the book will help you observe the antics of the unenlightened ego as it allows anger, greed, desire, pride, delusion, jealousy, and all the members of their "family circle" to cramp your feeling, pollute your heart, and create a web of negative karmas. Through the warm light of Swamiji's wisdom, you will be able to conquer these "enemies of the soul" with the weapons of compassion, cheerfulness, sincere introspection and undaunted self-effort.

In the second portion of the book, Swamiji gives insight into the process of converting normal feeling *(bhavana)* into spiritual feeling *(bhava)*. When spiritual feeling blossoms, Divine Love rises like the full moon and a devotee, having shed the veils of illusion, becomes one with God. There is nothing so sublime as a heart permeated by Divine awareness—a heart that is like a golden cup overflowing with ever-increasing Divine Love and Bliss. Undoubtedly, this book will prove to be a fountain-source of inspiration and strength for all who read it.

With *The Art of Positive Feeling* as your trusted companion, may you be led to the highest communion with God and enjoy a dynamic awareness of the Divine Presence at all times!

—*Swami Lalitananda*

This publication is dedicated:

CONTENTS

Author Sri Swami Jyotirmayananda

I

TRIUMPHING
OVER THE
ENEMIES OF THE SOUL

INTRODUCTION

Every human being has within himself a fount of inexhaustible strength and joy, because he is essentially the Divine Self. But due to wrong ways of thinking and feeling, man acquires various weaknesses which do not allow him to develop his inner potentiality. These weaknesses or impurities in the mind obscure the majesty of the Self as clouds in the sky obscure the brilliance of the sun.

The soul has six dangerous enemies, referred to as *shad-ripus*. These impurities, which are also referred to as *vikaras*, are *kama* (desire for sense-pleasures in general, passion in particular), *krodha* (anger), *lobha* (greed), *moha* (delusion, infatuation), *mada* (pride), and *matsarya* (jealousy). *Matsarya* is also referred to as *irshya* and *asuya*. With a slight variation they all mean jealousy in different forms.

These six interrelated impurities or vices, which actually include all negative qualities that plague human personality, are considered the *ripus*—enemies from one's very childhood, indeed enemies from many incarnations. As long as these enemies are not conquered, one cannot enjoy real prosperity or peace in life nor attain enlightenment. Thus, it must become the challenge—as well as the delight—of every aspirant to find those debilitating weaknesses and endeavor to remove them in order to awaken within himself the glorious vistas of spiritual unfoldment.

An Ancient View

In the Vedic literature, there is an intriguing verse which sheds some ancient light on these enemies of the soul:

"O Indra, may you crush by your thunderbolt the demon that moves in the form of an owl, an owl's young one, a dog, a *chakravaka* or ruddy goose, an eagle, and a vulture."
(Atharva Veda 8/4/22 and Rigveda 7/6/104)

What is the demon in the form of an owl? *Moha* or delusion. An owl cannot see during the day when other animals can see. Thus the owl is a symbol for a person that is blinded by delusion. A person overcome by *moha* can see only within the range of his egoistic feeling, but beyond that he is blind.

What is the demon in the form of an owl's young one? Jealousy or *matsarya*. Jealousy thrives in the absence of the light of rationality, reason. If you were to understand another person's life with penetrating vision, you would realize that there is nothing in that life to be jealous about. Everyone's life in this world of relativity has severe shortcomings. Thus, being jealous of someone for any apparent form of prosperity is usually totally irrational. That irrational envy, born of delusion, is the offspring of the owl of *moha.*

What is the demon that comes in the form of a dog? This demon is *krodha* or anger. When dogs fight they are totally unable to control themselves. You may teach your dog all types of lessons in training school, but when another dog challenges him for food, for example, he loses his temper completely.

The demon that comes in the form of the *chakravakra* or ruddy goose is *kama* or desire. This animal is well-known for its amorous courtship. The demon that soars in the form of an eagle is *mada* or egoistic pride. Finally, the demon in the form of a vulture is *lobha* or greed. Seized by greed, one does not have any discrimination. He is driven to possess and devour everything, just as a vulture eats all types of rubbish without any reservations.

Indra, in this context, is God, the Almighty. An aspirant seeks the blessings of God for the destruction of all these enemies of the soul.

An aspirant must reflect deeply—but with a generous sense of humor—upon this Vedic satire of human weaknesses. Due to his own shortcomings, does he really want to be as uncontrolled as an angry dog, as absurd as an amorous goose, and as greedy and undiscriminating as a vulture? Unfortunately, wrong ways of thinking and feeling often make human beings less virtuous—rather than more elevated—than their animal counterparts. However, with persistent introspection and sincere self-effort, every person can become the embodiment of Divine bliss and perfection that he is intended to be.

DESIRE
(KAMA)

The Sanskrit word *kama* has a number of different meanings. In one context, *kama* is the name given in the *Vedas* to one of the four *purushartas* or values that every individual must attend to in life. These include *dharma* (ethical value), *artha* (material value), *kama* (vital value), and *moksha* (spiritual value).

In relation to the *purushartas, kama* refers to the desire to establish joyous relationships with family members, friends, and other people around you in society. In an ideal plan of life, one should establish meaningful social relationships *(kama)* and secure material wealth *(artha)* while being ever-rooted in *dharma* (the ethical value of life.) One should then use his social and material wealth for intensifying his *dharma* and for moving towards *moksha* or liberation.

In such an ideal plan of life, the desires involved in *kama* and *artha* have a healthy and important role to play. However, in a disbalanced and aberrant society, this ideal plan is ignored and *kama* and *artha* become ends in themselves and are not regulated by *dharma* as they should be. Such unregulated *kama* and *artha* eventually generate negative impressions in the unconscious which lead to increasing stress, grief and frustration.

Further insight into *kama* or desire comes from a study of the three *gunas*, or modes of the mind: *sattwa, rajas* and *tamas*. A mind that is *tamasic* is characterized by delusion, dullness and negativity. When desire mixes with *tamas*, the result is the worst and crudest desire possible—desire for revenge, for harm to come to others, etc. When the mind is *rajasic*, it becomes externalized, distracted, restless, and gives rise to desires for more wealth, fame, power and many vanities of life. A *satwic* mind is filled with harmony, goodness and purity. The desires that arise when the mind is pervaded by *sattwa* are desires for good association, for reading scriptures, for having simplicity in life so that one can devote more mental energy to spiritual pursuit. *Satwic* desire is not harmful; rather, it is essential for spiritual progress.

Therefore, when we are studying the impurities of the mind and how to remove them, the form of *kama* that we are targeting is desire that is opposed to *dharma* (the basic ethical value of life), desire in general which is unduly *rajasic* and tamasic, and thus opposed to your spiritual movement, and desire in particular which is referred to as passionate desire.

Breaking the Fetters of Desire

Most human desires are expressions of ignorance and imperfection. Therefore, the pursuit of those desires is characterized by pain, frustration and failure. A mind infested by desires cannot rest in peace.

Desires are much like a net in which human consciousness is trapped. The bird of the human soul wishes to fly into the regions of freedom, but caught in the net of desires, it suffers untold miseries.

All miseries and afflictions proceed from desires. The external and internal conditions of life are manifestations of your desires. A person seeking peace, prosperity, Self-realization and immortality must learn the art of studying, purifying, and sublimating his desires.

Every unfulfilled and frustrated desire brings to the unconscious an impression of tension. With each impression of tension a portion of willpower is locked up. Thus, the more one desires, the less he is able to execute thoughts into actions. The more one desires, the less he is able to enjoy inner peace and tranquility.

Desire manifests in two forms, unconscious and conscious. Unconscious desires are known as vasanas or subtle desires. Very often people do not know their own subtle inclinations, and, while they consciously endeavor to build the pillars of peace and raise the mansion of spiritual prosperity and glory, they unconsciously create obstacles through the perpetuation of anger, hatred, egoism and attachment to worldly values. Torn between these conflicts of the conscious and the unconscious, human will is unable to work effectively toward the acceleration of one's evolution.

The Fisherwomen and the Flowers

Sri Ramakrishna Paramahamsa told a parable to illustrate the illusion created by human desires. Once three fisherwomen were returning home, but since it had become late, they decided to ask for a place to sleep at a house along the way. The owner of the house wanted to be as hospitable as possible, so when he prepared a place for them to sleep he decorated the room with jasmine, rose, queen-of-the-night and other fragrant flowers.

After tossing fitfully from side to side for an hour, one of the fisherwomen said, "What a foul smell! I cannot sleep at all!" Another fisherwoman, having the same problem, said, "I have an idea. Let us put our fishing nets over our noses, and then sprinkle them with water so that we may breathe in the wonderful fragrance of fish and shut out that foul smell." Having done so, they all slept peacefully.

Even so, human beings could abide in the fragrant mansion of the Lord amongst Divine flowers of virtues. However, instead they maintain the mask of desires and shut out the heavenly fragrance. Instead of resting blissfully in peaceful surrender, they prefer the fishy foulness of worldly vanities.

Do not act like those fisherwomen. Learn to renounce your inner attachments to worldly things that are mortal and perishable. Learn to be attached to God, the Immortal Being within. Thus you can enjoy the heavenly fragrance that never fades and experience the bliss that never diminishes.

Silence the Hissing Snake of Desire

So many people have no relaxation in their eyes or peace in their heart. Their lives are filled with grief. Like a snake hissing in the chambers of the heart, unfulfilled desire emits the poison of grief and agony.

One should develop a profound understanding that desires for the world cannot be satisfied by plunging into worldly enjoyments. The desire to drink cannot be cured by drinking day and night. The desire to gamble will not cease if you frequent casino tables every night. The desire for worldly pleasures will not terminate if you indiscriminately indulge in them day and night. The fact is, the more one runs after worldly pleasures, the more one's desires increase.

A fire burns only more fiercely when oil is poured into it; so too, a desire bursts into insurmountable proportions when you pour worldly impressions into your mind by thoughtlessly pursuing the desire. Lord Krishna describes this situation in the second chapter of the *Gita*: "By constantly thinking of an object, one becomes attached to the object. From attachment there arises desire. When the desire to possess the object is obstructed, one develops anger. Anger causes loss of reason. Loss of reason leads to loss of memory, and the loss of memory causes one's destruction."

While desires spell poverty and pain, aspiration for God-realization brings a harvest of spiritual wealth and joy. Those who are rid of desires and are established in the Self are like an ocean that remains unaffected by the rivers pouring into it. Such is the consciousness of sages, who experience objects and circumstances and yet remain ever-unaffected by them.

It Is Attachment
That Leads to Pleasure and Pain

Consider the example of a man who sees a new car in a showroom. His thinking of it again and again leads him to become attached to it and arouses a desire to possess that car. Ultimately he buys it and the car becomes a part of him, as it were. If anything goes wrong with it, he is personally affected. He becomes glued to the car through attachment, and he may even give his car a pet name. But then later, after he sells the car, even if he hears that it has been totalled in an accident, he remains unaffected.

This should illustrate how it is not the object, but the attachment to it, that causes pleasure or pain. Attachment does not reside in any object, but in the mind. If you are rid of attachment, you become the real master.

Happiness Cannot Be Secured Externally

Human beings always try to reach out and secure whatever people, places and things seem to promise them happiness. In so doing, they are tricked again and again by one grand illusion after another. As an example, suppose a friend of yours goes on a vacation to Hawaii. Early in the morning, he sits by the ocean and the sun is shining on the waves, and everything seems so bright and peaceful that his mind becomes calm and he feels overwhelmed with joy.

Lacking training in philosophy, your friend begins to feel that that spot where he sat by the sea is uniquely special and has the power to bring him untarnished happiness at all times. Soon his mind tells him, "You have enough money. Why don't you buy a property right here? Everyday you could come and sit by the beach and enjoy the beauty as intensely as you are enjoying it now."

Hearing these inner whispers, your friend's mind flares up with intense desire. He thinks, "Without that happiness, life is empty. This is what I must have." Quickly this one idea commands his single-minded concentration. He rushes to a real estate office, starts investigating properties and their values, and then actually purchases a property by the sea.

With the land in hand, he now sets about building a house, furnishing it, and landscaping with all his mental and physical energy and material resources. With these tasks underway, he then goes again to sit beside the sea at sunrise. Does he enjoy the beauty as he did in his first experience?

Much to his dismay, as he sits watching the waves he starts to think about all the red-tape he has had to cut through to get the property; about how much money is left in the bank and how he is going to pay the mortgages; about how he is going to avoid the damage caused by the salty wind that comes to his house and destroys all his metallic fixtures; about what to do when the next storm comes; about how to defend his house against robbers and vandals. With all these thoughts, he discovers that he has lost all his happiness and serenity!

Your friend could have avoided all that work and ensuing disappointment with a little philosophical understanding. Happiness doesn't come from outside. Each time your mind becomes calm and you feel happy, it is because the joy of the Self within is reflecting in the lake of your mind. Enjoy your happy experiences, but always remind yourself that the joy came from within your own heart, from within your innermost Self, which is God. In devotional terms, remind yourself that all comes to you from God. In Vedantic terms, remind yourself that all is God, nothing but God. You are yourself nothing but the Divine Self, and it is by turning to your own inner Self that you experience happiness.

When you experience a moment of joyous contentment in life, do not obey your senses blindly as if they were the master with a whip and you were only a slave. Give yourself some breathing room, a moment for reflection. Understand that the happiness you experience in the realm of senses is a form of illusion and do not rush to try to secure it forever.

If you must pursue objects, do it knowingly. Understand profoundly that happiness is not coming from them. If you keep company with a thief knowingly, then there is little harm. If you keep company with a thief unknowingly, then you are going to be hurt intensively.

The Rich Man and the Thief

A humorous story is told about a rich man who was traveling on a train. After departure, another man entered into the same compartment. He was a thief and the rich man knew it. Soon the rich man made friends with the thief without revealing to the thief that he knew about his criminal intentions.

Each time the rich man had to go out, he secretly placed his money under the pillow of the thief. When the thief found himself alone, he looked around everywhere for the money, but, try as he might, he couldn't find it.

Time passed, the journey ended, and it was time for the men to go their separate ways. The thief, with humility, approached the rich man and said, "What a wonder! I saw your money, and whenever you went out I searched everywhere for it, but I couldn't find it. Please tell me your secret!" The rich man said, "You are a thief, but not a psychologist. I knew that you would look everywhere but under your very own nose. So I hid the money under your pillow."

The lesson to learn from this story is that if you are in the company of a thief, you must be more clever than he is so as not to be hurt. The objects of the world are like thieves. If we let them, they rob us of our peace of mind by leading us to believe that they are the source of happiness and that they will stay with us forever. However, if you are wise you recognize that happiness does not come from objects, and that objects are perishable and impermanent. Knowing these facts, you begin to control your desires.

Then what happens to that energy of desire? It turns into an energy of Divine love. Instead of desiring objects, you desire mental peace, liberation. *Kama*, when controlled and sublimated, becomes Divine love. It becomes *mumukshutwa*—aspiration for attaining Self-realization.

Chemically speaking, diamonds and coal are both nothing but carbon, but there is a big difference between the two. Desire for the world is like coal. Desire for attaining God-realization is like a diamond. Worldly desire can be transformed into spiritual aspiration—just as mere coal is transformed into diamonds—when a constant effort is directed to control *kama* and to redirect it in a proper way.

The Trammels of Ninety-Nine

Another parable is told to demonstrate how desire is the great enemy of peace:

There was once a blacksmith who labored hard, but enjoyed his work immensely and always sang joyfully as he worked. When his rich neighbor heard that singing, he became extremely jealous. "How can it be," he thought to himself, "that with all my wealth, I can't even sleep due to worries and anxiety, and yet my poor neighbor is always so happy? Though he works so hard, hammering iron sheets close to a hot fire, still he enjoys his life and his work!" Unable to bear this situation a moment longer, the jealous neighbor thought and thought, and then came up with a simple plan.

Putting his scheme into effect, the neighbor secretly threw a bag containing ninety-nine dollars into the shop of the blacksmith. When the blacksmith entered his shop, he found the bag and wondered how it had got there. Unable to solve the mystery, he decided to keep the money and make good use of it.

Then the idea came into his mind, "It is only one dollar less than a hundred. It would have been nice if it was a hundred." So the next day he worked hard and, instead of just earning one dollar, he brought the total up to one hundred and twenty four. Then he thought to himself, "If the amount I had was one dollar more, it would be an even mathematical amount." So the next day he worked hard again, and the pattern continued: always needing a little more to make a nice round figure.

As the days passed, the blacksmith lost the peace and joy with which he used to work and there were no more songs. Of course, the neighbor was delighted because his plan had worked out just as he had hoped!

One day the blacksmith suddenly realized that he was becoming sick, weak and restless. Then he thought to himself, "All the trouble started from that ninety-nine." With a great sense of relief, he gathered that money and threw it over to the rich man's place, thinking that he could surely make good use of it.

In the Hindi language, there is a proverb that was inspired by this story: "Do not be entangled by ninety-nine." The moment you get caught by the illusion of needing more of something to be happy you become entangled — like the blacksmith — in a joyless pursuit.

Desires for things which are perishable are full of vanity. Desire Self-realization alone. Desire the development of spiritual values and virtues. Desire the betterment of humanity. Desire to become desireless.

Don't Be Trapped by Your Desires

In some parts of India, monkeys are trapped by a clever device. A jar with a narrow neck is filled with fruit and placed in a spot that monkeys frequent. Attracted by the fruit, a monkey puts his hand into the jar and grabs the fruit. Then having made his hand into a fist, he cannot take his hand out since the neck of the jar is too narrow. He can easily let the fruit go and release his hand, but he lacks this sense due to his desire to possess the fruit, and is caught.

Even so, human consciousness puts its hand into the narrow jar of egoism in order to catch the fruits of worldly enjoyments with the fingers of desire. Open your hand and let the fruit go. You will be released from the narrow prison of embodiment. You will realize, "I am all that exists. I am the eternal, infinite Truth."

Renounce worldly desires by serving humanity, by developing devotion and by practising profound enquiry. Let your mind be a channel of Divine Will. Perform actions with a sense of dedication to God.

When your heart if purified, it will become filled with sublime desires—desires that are expressions of Divine Will for the good of humanity. These desires do not bind or entrap the soul. Rather, they are like heavenly flowers blowing freely in the breeze, spreading their sublime fragrance everywhere.

PASSIONATE DESIRE

Every religion speaks of the importance of overcoming lustful passion. However, the Yogic scriptures have given a profound insight into this process by detailing the mystic practice of *brahmacharya*.

What is Brahmacharya?

Brahmacharya literally means "living and moving in *Brahman*—the Absolute, the Divine Self"—and in its highest form, *brahmacharya* implies being established in the awareness, "I Am *Brahman*." However, from a relative point of view, *brahmacharya* consists of restraining and sublimating the sex-urge.

Brahmacharya, in the most restricted sense, implies control and sublimation of sex energy through the practice of celibacy and restraint of sex-pleasures. Generally, therefore, people think of a *brahmachari* as a young person or a monk who is celibate and unmarried.

In ancient India the sages divided a human lifetime into four 25-year stages or *ashramas*. According to this system, people were to spend the first twenty-five years in *brahmacharya ashrama* (student life), the second in *grihastha ashrama* (householder or married life), the third in *vanaprastha ashrama* (a retired stage devoted to practice of austerity and teaching others in forest schools) and the fourth in *sanyasa ashrama* (renunciation).

This ancient system provided that students who were below the age of twenty-five should devote their time and energy to intensive study under the guidance of a guru or teacher. To enhance the power of this educational experience, they were enjoined not to enter into sex relationships and urged to remain celibate until the householder phase of life began after age twenty-five. That ideal of discipline was intended to prevent young people from being caught up in the frivolities of sex as a result of their vital, physical and nervous urges and to free their energy for handling the responsibilities of that portion of their life.

Although the practice of sexual restraint by students and the vow of celibacy adopted by monks and renunciates are a very important aspect of *brahmacharya*, they signify only a restricted understanding of this very great ideal.

Whether a person is married or unmarried, the biological demand of life, the instinctive urge for procreation and for passion, continues to assert itself. It influences all people, young and old, in all stages of life, and a complete mastery over it requires the same kind of profound understanding necessary for conquering the subtle roots of violence in human personality. Therefore, *brahmacharya*, in a broader sense, is to be understood and practised by people at all stages of life, whether married or unmarried.

Mere externals are not an indicator of one's advancement in *brahmacharya*. An unmarried person can be more preoccupied with sexuality than one who is married and may have many thoughts and fantasies about passion swirling within his mind.

A married couple with children, on the other hand, may reach a level of understanding in which they realize that sex is not an end in itself, and they may learn to fulfill their sentiments on deeper levels and no longer rely on sex. In that case, their relationship becomes very profound and they are moving towards true *brahmacharya*.

In the deeper philosophical sense, *brahmacharya* implies control and sublimation of biological passion, leading to the recovery of a deeper perception of love. This deeper, infinitely inspiring and elevating love unites not just the sexes, but man with the universe, with all that exists. The ideal of *brahmacharya* asserts that a human being, whether male or female, is intrinsically the Self (*Brahman*), and his or her instinct to love will ultimately be completely fulfilled only in the state of Self-realization, wherein union with the Self-in-all is attained.

The Human Need for Communion and Creative Fulfillment

An inherent urge to create and to commune with all that exists operates in every personality. It is the essential longing of every soul, although most people are not consciously aware of this. The more familiar instinctive, biological urge to reproduce and to become involved in passionate relationships is merely a shadow of the intuitional demand of your soul to commune with all that exists.

That urge deep within for inner creativity and expansion of the soul can be fulfilled without entering into relationships, but only if one is spiritually evolved and possesses a highly intuitive intellect.

Without having produced children, you can feel the fulfillment of seeing all children as your own children. You can feel your own Self in all, without ever getting into any relationships of a selfish, physical nature. But it requires a supernormal mind, a saintly mind, for one to have this experience of spiritual unity.

Until one is evolved enough to experience true cosmic consciousness and Divine love, one needs interpersonal relationships and family involvements to help awaken the desire for such lofty forms of love. Nature awakens in you the idea of loving the Self — a love which is difficult to cognize — by enchanting you with the many easily understood varieties of love in the world: passionate love, parental love, love between friends, love between a teacher and a student, etc.

A human being must be creatively fulfilled. If one does not experience a deeper form of creativity on the mental and spiritual level, then nature forces him to fulfill the creative urge on the physical and instinctive planes.

In this process of your exploring the pleasures of the world in search of happiness and fulfillment, Nature does not seem to care what happens to your physical system. She subjects your body to repeated heights of passion and states of dissipation until your personality believes it has fulfilled the urge for passion and biological creativity. Deluded by illusory pleasure, it is possible to forget that you are not merely a biological personality, that you are a human being with the possibility of overcoming biological instinct and enjoying the blessings of intuitive understanding.

As you advance spiritually, you begin to enjoy intuitive expansion and discover a different form of creation — a creativity of consciousness, a creativity of the soul. The moment that creativity arises, the need for biological creativity is overcome. This is what is referred to as sex-sublimation in yogic terminology.

When the mental energy that pours down into the senses is controlled by intuitive understanding, your thoughts are clear, your mind is sensitive to the deeper harmony inherent in the world, and you enjoy a more profound joy in life. Sublimated sex energy — known in yogic terminology as *ojas shakti* — produces an extraordinary vitality in the human body and mind. A mind that vibrates with spiritual strength radiates an effulgence which gives a glow and luster to the entire personality. That magnetic effulgence has a powerful effect on others and helps them to perceive their own potential strength in a most inspiring and Divine way.

Compare that state of mind with the state of mind that arises in the height of passion. The mind overcome by passion is a tense and clouded mind, it depends helplessly on the objects of pleasure, and it is devoid of any real creativity.

When you compare the mind in these two states, you begin to understand the sweetness and the grandeur that arise due to mental expansion. This higher form of joy overcomes the mind's inclination towards lesser pleasures, and that is what is referred to as sex-sublimation or *brahmacharya*.

A Philosophical Look at Sexual Differences

Preoccupation with sex has its roots in body-identification: identifying yourself as a male or female. However, in reality, the innermost Spirit in a person is neither male nor female, and is unaffected by the characteristics of the physical body. Led by different *karmas*, an individual soul may incarnate as a male in one birth and as a female in another. Once you deeply understand that you are spirit, you are no longer enslaved by gender and, even in your lifetime, you overcome sex-consciousness as well as body identification itself.

When human beings see each other as bodies, they are putting each other in a degraded position. But when they see each other as spirit, it is very uplifting. The body may appear to be the most important thing about another person in the beginning of a relationship, but as your intellect matures you realize that the body is just a cloth. The spirit is beyond body, beyond sexes.

Men and women basically are sexless. They are spirits — not males or females. In the plane of spirit there are no sexes. However, in the process of evolution, there is a need for the soul to discover certain qualities of the mind, and that need polarizes itself in the form of male and female personalities. In the course of the soul's repeated incarnation, females have not been females all the time and males have not been males all the time. Their souls have assumed different personalities, male and female, as one incarnation has followed another.

Depending on and identifying with their biological structures, males and females consider themselves to be imperfect and incomplete without each another and they begin to relate themselves to each other in diverse ways, drawn by a powerful attractive force that they do not understand.

If that force is properly understood, it will lead to the practise of *brahmacharya* and a higher form of relationship. If that force is not properly understood, one is simply captured by the instinctive demands for biological procreation and passion.

Although you may be drawn to a partner by instinctive and karmic factors, gradually you must come to realize that the purpose of love and married

life is not merely the deriving of comfort and pleasure. Rather, partners in a healthy and meaningful
love relationship must learn to minimize their selfish demands for pleasure and become endowed with
increasing endurance, patience, self-sacrifice and
understanding. If they are able to do so, they are
promoting their mutual spiritual evolution and their
union will be glorified. If they do not, then their
union is simply an external show and will not lead to
real fulfillment and satisfaction.

Fidelity and the Purpose of Marriage

The Divine commandment of the Bible, "Be
fruitful and multiply," does not imply merely multiplying physically. It implies multiplying in consciousness.

If you make sexual pleasure predominant in a
marriage, then you are overlooking the central spiritual goal of marriage and practising a subtle but
significant form of infidelity as well. Fidelity is not as
simple as just being married and abstaining from
sexual relations with anyone other than your spouse.
If the love that exists between husband and wife has
not engendered an understanding of a Divine relation between them, if husband and wife depend
entirely on passionate confirmation of their love,
then that love is fraudulent.

A couple may stay together without any outward
infidelity, yet, since the perception of higher love

has not yet dawned, they will always be insecure in their relationship. Their love is simply a matter of attachment and entanglement, and in most cases, it will eventually fade.

Fidelity, then, is not merely external in a relationship. It implies that those who love each other are faithful to each other in their souls. It implies that they strive to acquire a profoundly mature understanding of what love really is.

One who practises *brahmacharya* understands that no form of loving relationship must exist solely as a means to pleasure. Pleasure does not refer just to sexual delight in this context. It refers to the mind's infatuation with all objects that are loved and with the delight that the relationships can bring.

This applies to the love between a child and his parents, to the love that exists between friends, to all forms of love that exist in human life. None of these loving relationships must be considered solely a means to pleasure, but they should become a means of elevation, upliftment and inspiration. Your love for another passes the Divine test if the one you love is led to elevation through your love. But if your love in any way degrades you and the person to whom your love is directed, there is a lack of true *brahmacharya*, a lack of true fidelity.

Real love will not be confined to family, nor to a few friends. It becomes universal, cosmic, without a shadow of sentimentality of a lower nature, without a shadow of enslavement to biological instinct or passion. This is the indescribably dynamic love which existed in the heart of Christ, in the heart of Buddha, in the heart of all sages and saints whose love continues to shine as a source of light and power for all.

True Love Sees the Beauty of the Spirit

A story is told about a prince who considered himself very handsome and sensuous. One day he saw a farmer girl and became enchanted by her beauty. He proposed to her, asking if she would marry him right away. Because the young lady was already in love with somebody else, she was not interested in the prince but she did not know how to reject him without making him angry. Then an idea entered her mind.

She told the prince that she needed a little time before she accepted his proposal, and asked him to come back the next day, when she would be ready to marry him. The prince left cheerfully, dreaming of returning the next day to claim his bride.

As soon as the prince departed, the clever young lady swallowed a powerful drug that rapidly made her ugly looking and deformed. So when the prince arrived the next day, in the place of the beautiful young woman he found a sad looking creature that he could hardly bear to look at. "Where is the beautiful lady that I saw yesterday?" he asked. She replied, "I am that woman who is to be your bride.

But I am just not feeling well right now." Horrified, the prince said, "You could never be my bride!" and, so saying, he rode hurriedly away.

Just as that prince could see only the external form of the woman, not the beauty of her spirit, so too, most romantic love is confined to the externalities of a person and is incredibly selfish. Therefore, when you find yourself drawn into a love relationship, you must ask yourself, "If my partner grows old and loses the beauty and charm of youth or is marred by an illness or accident, will I continue to love with the same intensity?" If the answer is "no," then that form of love is mere frivolity.

Meaningful love, no matter what form it takes, demands understanding, sacrifice, and patience. It demands that the people involved in the relationship mutually assist one another in rising to higher and higher planes of understanding and awareness. If they do not strive to elevate each other in this way, the relation will either break up, or it will become a source of great pain and frustration.

Thus, inspired by the natural urge to love and be loved, men and women of greater sensitivity can move from lesser levels of love to the most sublime. As their understanding advances, they begin to love the Supreme Self who is the Reality in all. This love of the Self does not disrupt human sentiments and relationships. Rather it renders them holy and infuses them with depth.

When Sex Becomes a Sin

The ideal of *brahmacharya* does not regard sex as a great shame and sin, but considers it as a creative force that should not be abused. The ideal of *brahmacharya* requires that your mind understand the implications and purpose of sex in your life, and the possibility of transcending and sublimating that force towards mental advancement. Sex can be a means to a deeper life if it is promoted with fidelity and understanding. But, if that deeper love is not in view, then sexual indulgence is mostly debilitating and degrading.

The misuse of sex implies a lack of *brahmacharya*. When sex is misused it becomes evil and can result in all types of vice and criminality. If a person's sexual desires are not fulfilled, his mind can be overcome by a tremendous restlessness that gives rise to egoism, pride, jealousy, anger, greed, and many other negative qualities in the human personality.

ANGER
(KRODHA)

Anger or *krodha* exists in many degrees, ranging from ordinary annoyance to intense, violent rage. Contempt, intolerance, vengeance, and hatred are all inseparably-related forms of *krodha*. Even those who are highly educated and apparently religious suffer from this malady.

If anger, hatred and revenge were to be taken away from the world, ninety-percent of the movie producers would go out of business. However, for those who want to enjoy the spiritual values of life and to attain true success, peace, and inner fulfillment, these terrible vices need to be eradicated.

Nothing is more degrading for an aspirant than to keep his mind burdened with the manifold forms of *krodha*. They darken the mirror of the mind, dissipate willpower, create illusions, waste mental energy, intensify negative karmas, promote chaos for oneself and others, and lead one to manifold forms of misery. Every effort must be directed by an aspirant towards the prevention as well as cure of this crippling disease of the astral body.

A Slave of My Slaves

An interesting story is told about Alexander the Great, whose guru was a devotee of Indian philosophy. One day the guru told Alexander, "If you go to India, conquer kingdoms if you must; but, of greater importance, visit a sage and, if possible, bring him back with you."

When Alexander reached India he followed the guru's advice and went to a well-known saint and introduced himself quite pompously. The saint didn't say anything nor bow his head, as everyone was supposed to do before the emperor. Alexander said, "Don't you know that I have conquered most of the world, and no one is greater than I? How is it that you don't give me respect?" The sage replied, "Because you are the slave of my slave."

"What do you mean?" demanded Alexander angrily. "I can cut you down with a sword." The sage laughed, "Do you think I am this body that you can cut down?" Alexander became quiet and asked for further explanation of the wise man's words. The sage said, "Well, you see, anger, hate, and greed are the greatest enemies and they are my slaves—and you are their slave. So you are the slave of my slaves."

What Causes Krodha?

Sometimes there is a certain rationality behind expressions of *krodha*—someone has actually hurt you in some way, inflicting injury on you physically or psychologically—and as a result you feel that the person should receive similar injury. But often people become angry and hateful for no reason at all due to the irrational functioning of intellect. Often this irrationality stems from psychological impressions gathered in childhood. During your childhood you may have encountered many deep frustrations and, because of that, many situations stir up memories that cause you to react inappropriately.

When one's life lacks a deeper goal, when one has not yet become interested in the project of discovering his or her inner Self and of being united with God, one becomes easily bored with life and seeks stimulation. Positive situations can stimulate the nervous system, but they are often hard to create. On the other hand, the mind has devised a way of easily creating negative situations through acts of anger and intolerance, which readily create dissension and disharmony.

The deeper roots of anger are impressions of dislike, or *dwesha*, in the unconscious mind. Impressions of like (*raga*) and dislike (*dwesha*) limit one's mental capacity and cause one to become agitated.

Due to contraction of consciousness, every frustrating situation makes you feel as if you are surrounded by walls, and there is no recourse but to get angry. At such moments you forget that such situations have come a thousand times and then have passed away. Becoming angry never was—and never will be—an effective and necessary solution.

Righteous Indignation?

Many aspirants make the mistake of justifying their bursts of anger as "righteous indignation." This terminology was applied to Jesus' display of anger in a temple. When he saw things were not being done in a righteous way, he threw everything around and showed his displeasure. Similarly, Krishna and Arjuna displayed a righteous and necessary form of anger in the Mahabharata War. Parents, too, have to be angry at times. If they became absolutely cool and calm they would not be able to discipline their children.

This type of anger is of a special nature and it has its proper place in life. Behind such anger there is a spiritual purpose, a project of compassion and love. It is love-backed anger.

However, an aspirant should not confuse this issue and justify every bout of anger as righteous indignation! Most angry situations are not righteous indignation. If your anger is truly purposeful, it will not deeply agitate your mind. It will not disturb the placidity of your reason. You will not lose your power of observation, nor your balance. Righteous anger is like a knife used by a skillful chef: you wield it to cut the vegetables, but you do not cut your fingers!

When Anger Gets out of Hand

Expressions of *krodha* begin within your own heart, but eventually affect not only your family, but all your relationships. They spread out into society, affecting many people, like sparks that lead to a conflagration of fire.

A Hindi poet once said, *"Avat gari ek hai, ulatat hot anek."* This literally means that if one car is coming down the road and due to some impediment it turns over, it will become many. That is, the accident will cause the car to break apart into numerous pieces. The verse contains a pun on the word *"gari,"* which means an abusive word as well as a car. Thus, the verse implies that if someone says just one abusive word to you and you react the same way, the whole situation will become a wreck of complications and get out of hand.

Just One Drop of Honey

To gain insight into the chaos that anger and its ramifications can cause, reflect on this humorous parable:

Once upon a time there was a honey vendor who went to a shop to sell his product. While he was negotiating the sale, one little drop fell on the floor without the vendor or the shopkeeper knowing it.

Within a few moments, a little lizard that was in the shop spotted the honey that dropped on the floor and started licking it. The shopkeeper's cat quickly spotted the lizard and pounced on it. Then a dog that had entered the shop with a customer got so exited that he broke away from his master's leash and attacked and injured the cat.

Needless to say, the shopkeeper became very angry; he grabbed a stick, banged the dog with it and broke its leg. This infuriated the dog's owner, who then smashed the shopkeeper over the head.

It just so happened that the shopkeeper had many friends and they all got wind of what was happening. The owner of the dog also had many friends and they too heard what was going on. So, lo and behold, there was a free-for-all! A tremendous fight broke out and the shop was ruined——all over a drop of honey.

That spilled drop of honey is like the spirit of *krodha,* which can cause absolute chaos. Anger and its ramifications disturb the harmony that is extremely important in life, creating tension and discord, hurting others as well as oneself.

The Poor Nose

Recall the humorous parable of a man whose monkey servant always fanned him while he was sleeping to drive away the flies. One day a fly persisted in buzzing around the master's nose and the monkey went on trying to drive the fly away. When that fly continued to come again and again, the monkey's mind was overwhelmed by frustration and clouded by the spirit of vengeance. So, he took a big rock and smashed it right on the fly. Unfortunately, the fly was right on the nose of the master! The fly flew off, as if mocking the monkey's vengeance, but the nose of the angry master just lay there throbbing with intense pain! Similarly, whenever you take recourse to vengeance, you may hurt yourself and those you love as well as those you feel deserve to be punished.

Controlling the Three-fold Expressions of Anger

Anger expresses in three ways: physical, verbal and mental. When an uncultured person becomes angry, he may pick up anything and bang it upon the head of the person who is the provoker of his anger. If one is more civilized, all he does is bang the telephone or slam the door shut. Both are physical expressions of anger, and both need to be controlled as the first step in the war against anger. Even though anger may linger mentally, and you may utter harsh words, at least let there be no physical expression of anger in your deeds.

The second step in controlling anger is to curtail its verbal expression. You may still be harboring anger in your mind at this stage, but strive to control your speech. This effort saves you from all the painful repercussions that result from having spoken harsh words. Whether your anger is rational or irrational, an uncontrolled tongue always leads to regret, repentance and wastage of energy. Therefore, verbal anger has to be controlled.

In the *Mahabharata*, Yudhishthira asks Bhishma, "What is one great quality that can enable a person to be successful anywhere in the world, in all projects?" Bhishma replied, "Mastery over the tongue. If you could stop expressing anger through your tongue, your success would be secured in all directions."

Finally, your ultimate goal is to eliminate ill will in your mind, to free yourself of the affliction of mental anger. Ideally, your mind should be so free of this affliction that you don't even recognize the evil done to you. But that requires a profound understanding of philosophy. To encourage yourself to reach this higher state of mental purity, reflect upon the following insights:

Anger Is Like a Boomerang || Whenever you sustain anger in your mind, you are hurting yourself. The one who is angry and the one to whom the anger is being directed both become degraded. The effect on the person to whom you are directing your anger varies according to that person's karma. If that person is vulnerable, then he will be affected. Otherwise, your anger will simply come back to you like a boomerang and hurt you with all its force.

If you send somebody to hell, you have also sent yourself there to babysit him. How would you know the person is actually suffering in Hell unless you are there to watch him? Out of anger, people curse each other, but they have really cursed themselves. The moment you send someone to Hell, you'd better get busy and pack your own suitcase for that long trip.

Every time you hold a grudge and intend to hurt another person by your thoughts or actions, you create a negative karma that keeps you in conjunction with that person in the future. You have to remain close to them in order to see the desire for revenge fulfilled!

***As You Sow,
So You Reap***
Develop insight into the law of karma. No one can hurt you unless your karma allows it. It is the impressions in your unconscious that draw negative situations to you. You have drawn those situations and circumstances to yourself by your actions and thoughts in the past. Therefore, if you don't want to reincarnate again and again into a world of bitter circumstances, you should not hold any grudge against others. Rather, hold a grudge against yourself for creating the karmic process that has brought you pain—and consider others as Divine agents reminding you of that error. In so doing, you will develop spiritual qualities within yourself and become a saint, rather than a perpetrator of violence.

Day by day you must be watchful that the negative qualities that might lead you to acts of angry revenge are not encouraged in your personality. If you are irritable and insensitive, if you are not patient and adaptable in your relationships with others, if you are intolerant towards other people and can't wait to listen to what they have to say before you pass your judgments, you are sowing the seeds of negative karmas which will bear bitter fruits in the future.

You will eventually find yourself in situations where no one will be able to tolerate your behavior, your personality traits, your weaknesses, or even your looks. Your very presence will become a source of disharmony. When you crave compassion, you will find that people around you are not compassionate. Then you will wonder how it is that the world has become so cruel and insensitive! At that time you will not realize that you made the world around you as difficult as it is.

Spiritual virtues have a special magic about them: when you develop them within your personality, similar qualities proceed from others and are directed towards you. If you are compassionate towards others, compassion from an external source comes to you in a time of need.

It Could Have Been Worse! In confronting life's annoying and difficult situations, one has to constantly reflect upon the relativity of things. When things seem bad, remember that they could always have been worse—and give thanks to God that they were not!

Once a disciple appeared before Buddha and said, "I want to go home to pay back to society some evils I did before." In his early days, the disciple had been a robber and had caused a lot of hurt. Now as a *sanyasi* (renunciate), having attained a state of purity, he said that he would like to face those people from whom he had run away before, and thereby exhaust his negative karma.

Buddha said, "Suppose you go there and people don't appreciate your presence? Suppose they insult you, or they laugh at you?" He said, "I will say to myself, 'Thanks to the Buddha within me that they are simply saying insulting words. They are not beating me, they are not pelting stones at me.'"

Buddha responded, "Suppose they do pelt stones at you?" He said, "Then I will thank God they are pelting stones at me and thereby repaying me for what I have done to them so the account will be cleared." Buddha then said, "Suppose they don't just pelt you, but kill you?" He said, "Then they would have released me from the bondage of embodiment."

Why Waste Precious Energy? Life is short, and must be well-utilized for a higher purpose. Do not allow the mind to acquire the habit of being angry over little things. Be introspective. Look within yourself again and again. If you create dissension and tension during the first half of the day, spend the rest of the day worrying about the repercussions, and then the next day struggle to remedy the situation, think of all the time and energy you have wasted.

Conserve your energy for the central project of your life—the attainment of Self-realization. In the short duration of your life, you have this tremendous task to accomplish, and it requires that you should be as enduring, patient, forgiving, and broad-hearted as possible.

Patients Require Patience You must realize that an evil doer is a sick person. If a doctor is caring for a sick patient, how will he deal with that person? If the patient, due to illness, is throwing things around, the doctor will try to save himself from injury—but he will not start throwing things back in anger. He will wait for an opportunity to help the patient. Similarly, you should have that type of attitude in dealing with all those who seek to harm you.

Love Even Your Enemies Terminating anger implies promoting the opposite of anger—forgiveness, love, patience, endurance, understanding. Even in cases where the mind seems to direct hatred on a rational basis, one must place before himself the ideal taught by Buddha and Jesus, and endeavour to develop goodwill and compassion even towards those who are bent upon harming him.

Remember the sayings of Lord Jesus: "Ye have heard that it hath been said, 'Thou shalt love thy neighbor, and hate thine enemy.' But I say unto you, love your enemies, bless them that curse you, do good to them that hate you, and pray for them which despitefully use you, and persecute you, that ye may be the children of your Father in heaven." (Matthew

5:43-45) Directing love and goodwill even towards those who are crude and inimical is indeed supernormal. But unless one upholds this saintly ideal, he cannot rise beyond the normal level of human consciousness.

Do not develop an internal grudge when you are harmed. Revenge leads you nowhere. If someone has inflicted pain upon you and you have suffered, there is nothing you can do to undo that pain. Plotting to have the evildoer experience equal or greater pain does not remedy the pain you have already experienced. A nobler approach is for you to enable the person to understand his error through the higher power of love, endurance and patience.

In the *Ramayana*, Tulasidas says that a saintly personality is like a sandlewood tree. If you strike an ax against the sandlewood tree, what does the tree do to the ax? It simply makes the ax fragrant. Similarly, if a crude person comes to harm a saintly person, that saint radiates a fragrance that can turn the evildoer into a saint. This ideal of endurance, forbearance and compassion must always be held in view.

Flowers For Thorns

Saint Kabira has given the following profound advice: If a person plants thorns on your pathway, do not go to his home and do the same in return. Instead, stealthily go to his place and plant all the best flowers there. If you do so, a miracle will occur. The thorns that the person has planted to hurt you will become flowers of blessings, and the flowers that you sow for him will prick his heart in such a way that he will begin to repent for the evil he has done, and as a result, there will be a transformation within him. Thus, while crude people retaliate in a negative way, retaliation by a saintly personality is of a positive nature and has profound effects for the development of virtue.

Breaking the Cycles of Violence

No negative sentiment, especially hatred, can ever be appeased by enjoying or indulging in that sentiment. Suppose you have hated a person for some time. Would seeing that person revenged upon in a most miserable manner rid your mind of that hatred? Would you be free of it? No! The more you hate and seek revenge on that person, the more you fear that person's revenge in the future. Therefore, your hatred becomes more and more reinforced.

Buddha once found two factions of his disciples quarrelling among themselves. When he saw that day by day their hatred was being sustained, he told them the following parable:

Long ago in Benares there was a King named Brahmadatta. Because he was ambitious and wanted to expand his kingdom, Brahmadatta conquered the small kingdom of Kaushala that was ruled by another King named Dirgheti. To secure his rulership of that kingdom, Brahmadatta decided to kill the conquered King and Queen so that they could never rise up against him to regain the kingdom.

However, before the plot could be carried out, Dirgheti and his wife escaped. Eventually they went into hiding in Benares, assuming a disguise and living in the home of a potter who was their friend. They lived there with a sense of security and eventually had a son named Dirghayu. Dirghayu was a promising young boy and when he reached the age of sixteen he was sent out by his parents to be better educated.

During this time when the son was away, a barber recognized the disguised Dirgheti. Hoping greedily to receive a reward for the information, the barber quickly reported his whereabouts to King Brahmadatta. Eager to destroy his old enemy, the King sent his soldiers to the house of the potter and Dirgheti and his wife were taken away to await their fate.

On the day of the execution, a crowd gathered at the site where the grim event was to take place, and in that crowd was Dirghayu. When the former king, Dirgheti, saw his son coming towards him, he became terribly afraid that the youth would do something to reveal himself before Brahmadatta and be executed as well. To warn the boy, the father shouted to him, "Oh my son, do not look long, do not look short. Hatred is not appeased by hatred, but by nonhatred alone."

King Brahmadatta did not understand this strange riddle, and although he knew there was a son somewhere among the crowd, he could not find him. Thus, before the eyes of their child, King Dirgheti and his wife were executed, and Dirghayu was left with terrible pain in his heart.

As he grew up, Dirghayu became an expert in handling elephants, and as a result, he was asked to work in the royal elephant stable. There Dirghayu used to play on a flute so melodiously that one day the King heard him from the window and was enchanted by the song. King Brahmadatta asked to have the young man brought before him, and found him to be endowed with excellent qualities. Dirghayu became a close counsellor and companion of the King, and wherever the King went, he took Dirghayu with him. King Brahmadatta never realized that this young man he liked so much was the son of the former king and queen he had executed, and he never suspected that Dirghayu was always waiting for the perfect opportunity to kill him in revenge.

Then one day that opportunity came. During a hunting excursion the king strayed away from the main army as he rode in his chariot along with Dirghayu. Due to the hot weather, the King became very tired and Dirghayu suggested that they rest in the cool shade of the trees. So they got down from the chariot, and Dirghayu laid the head of the King on his thigh and asked him to relax there for awhile.

When the King fell sleep, Dirghayu saw the opportunity he had been waiting for. Nobody was around and the King was completely in his power! However, as he unsheathed his sword, he remembered the words of his father—and then quickly he put the sword away.

Suddenly the King opened his eyes, and with great fear, trembling all over, he said, "I had a terrible dream." "What did you dream?" asked Dirghayu. The King replied, "I have been dreaming that the son of the royal couple I executed is going to avenge on me. In my dream I saw that son near me with a sword in his hand, ready to kill me."

As the King was telling Dirghayu about his dream, Dirghayu again drew his sword and said, "I am that son and I am going to kill you." Shocked and frightened, the King replied, "Please don't kill me." "Likewise, don't kill me either," said Dirghayu. "I am as much in fear of you as you are in fear of me. So let us make a truce not to kill each other." "Verily so," responded the King. "I pledge our enduring friendship."

Then the King, having recovered from the shocking situation, asked Dirghayu, "What was the meaning of the message given by your father at the time of his death?" Dirghayu explained, "'Do not look long' means do not sustain hatred for a long time. 'Do not look short' means do not act hastily. If I was hasty, I would have run the sword against your throat and then I would have been killed by your people. Then my people would go after you and yours, and the chain would continue. However, if I extend forgiveness to you for what you did, and you extend fearlessness to me, the cycle of violence will be broken."

After telling this story to his disciples, Buddha concluded by reminding them that it is by nonhatred alone—by acts of love and understanding—that hatred can be overcome. This type of philosophy promotes world peace, as opposed to the philosophy whereby hatred is perpetuated and often sustained from lifetime to lifetime, causing endless grief.

Soap and Water for the Mind

It must be well understood that if you did not encounter gross personalities, people who are crooked and difficult, there would be no evolution. No one would become a saint if there were no demoniac personalities.

God, in His infinite wisdom, has provided all types of people to interrelate with each other for the purpose of learning and growth. By their inspiring example and influence, saintly people go on urging those who are not saintly to advance spiritually. On the other hand, by their gross nature, and by continually creating difficulty for others, demoniac personalities go on urging the saints to attain even loftier states of perfection. Therefore, you should not look upon the unsaintly personalities as having no place in the world.

As Kabira says, "If you find someone who insults you constantly, appreciate that person and give them a place in your home, for that person will purify your mind without the help of soap and water."

If you want to increase your physical strength, you may have to go to a gym or a health spa and pay a lot of money. However, if mental strength is what you are after, the project is a simple one. Simply cherish everyone who constantly criticizes you and never allows you a moment's peace, and do whatever you can to keep them around, for he or she affords you the opportunity of gaining immense mental strength by keeping your mind alert, your will effective, and your introspection keen—and you don't have to pay a cent for their services.

Welcoming Durvasa

The Hindu scriptures have given us a wealth of colorful stories about the "angry sage"—Durvasa. The following story is one of the most intriguing because it reveals the highest philosophical understanding that can propel an aspirant high above the petty realms of anger. When one remembers Durvasa's extraordinary antics and their mystic implications, the war against anger becomes almost delightful!:

Once upon a time an imposing looking *brahmin* appeared in Dwaraka, where Lord Krishna had his palace. He was wearing tattered clothes, and carried a stick in his hand. He had a strange mustache and beard, and was unusually thin and tall. Whenever he saw anyone he announced, "Here am I. My name is Durvasa. Who would give me hospitality? There is, however, this condition: if you make the slightest mistake in attending on me, I may destroy you with my anger. So knowing this, is there anyone who would dare give me hospitality and who would risk causing me annoyance?"

Everyone was afraid and, therefore, no one came forward to welcome Durvasa. Seeing this, Lord Krishna himself came forward and said, "Oh Sage, I will offer my hospitality and I will consider it a great privilege to do so."

Thus, Durvasa came to stay at Krishna's palace, and because his demands were beyond human imagination he created tremendous inconvenience for Krishna's royal household. In one sitting he could eat up as much food as could be consumed by hundreds of people. At another time, although the royal chefs might have prepared all types of wonderful dishes, he would eat nothing—just pick up a grain and throw everything else away. Without telling anyone he would suddenly leave, and then he would reappear at any time, even in the middle of the night. All of a sudden he would start laughing for no reason, or start crying for no reason. Once he set all his bedding and clothes on fire and slipped away from the scene. Despite all this, Krishna continued to attend to the demands of the sage, and had his entire family do likewise.

On one particular day during his visit Durvasa came and said "O Krishna, I want to eat *keer* (rice pudding) immediately." Accordingly, wonderful pudding was quickly prepared. He took a little of that *kheer* and said, "O Krishna, this is *prasad* (sanctified food). Smear it all over your body." Without any objection, Krishna took handfuls of the pudding and smeared it all over his body.

While this was going on, Krishna's Queen, Rukmini, smiled. Durvasa's attention was drawn to that smile, and he immediately commanded that Rukmini be yoked to a chariot and pull the chariot just like a horse. Rukmini looked at Krishna for help, but when he didn't say anything, she knew that the order would have to be obeyed. So she allowed herself to be yoked to the chariot and began to pull it with all her might. Then Durvasa took a whip and started whipping her, and since Rukmini was not at all accustomed to this type of treatment, she faltered and fell. Durvasa simply shouted at her and when she completely collapsed, he jumped out of the chariot and went on by foot, as if in great anger. Krishna went after him, trying to appease the Sage, his body besmeared with *kheer*. "O Lord," Krishna said to Durvasa, "Be pleased. Do not be angry with us."

Then Sage Durvasa said to Krishna, "Oh Krishna, you have passed the test. You have conquered anger. I have not seen even a single flaw in your conduct and I am immensely pleased. As a result of pleasing me, you will become the source of attraction for all living beings, the object of infinite love. As long as the world exists, people will sing your glory. You will be the best in the three worlds, dear to all. All the things that I have broken and destroyed will become as they were and better. All the hurt that I have inflicted upon Rukmini will be gone and she will be perfectly healthy and brighter than ever, and wherever you have smeared the *kheer* on your body you will become invulnerable. Thus saying, Sage Durvasa blessed Rukmini and, having expressed his great joy, he vanished.

Durvasa is the personification of trouble and pain, of annoying situations that come in human life. Durvasa comes to visit everyone day by day in the form of situations that cause frustration and rob one of patience. For an aspirant, handling those situations is like welcoming Durvasa—and he must be careful not to incur his displeasure! If you are handling difficult situations with patience, if even in the most agonizing situations you hold your reason in balance, then you are appeasing Durvasa—that aspect of God who is testing you.

The ill-temper of Durvasa is based upon a Divine meaning and purpose. Though apparently so irrational, he is working out the Divine will through the deeper movement of his personality, leading people to their spiritual goal. Naturally, on that path leading to Self-realization, endurance must reach the highest level possible in an individual.

Troubles in human life arise from many sources. Ninety-percent of those troubles come from human sources. While interacting with other people, you often find that what you hold as most desirable is not held as desirable by your relative or friend. Then you see your expectations crushed. In turn you become the crusher of others' expectations. Durvasa is acting mutually among people. Sometimes you become Durvasa for someone else, sometimes someone else becomes Durvasa for you. Fortunately, one does not encounter Durvasa in his entirety at any one moment—if that were so one would explode. If all the annoying situations were to present themselves at once, one could not survive. Therefore, they are given to you little by little.

In those human interactions in which different types of personalities clash, tensions sometimes linger for a long time, and yet an aspirant should adopt tremendous patience. This is especially true in situations which seem irrational. As Krishna's behavior in the story illustrates, when you follow the path of controlling the mind and ego, rationality or irrationality does not matter. Your project is simply to develop the necessary self-control. You cannot sit back and say, "Oh, I could have controlled my mind under other circumstances, but this situation is too irrational for that!" Krishna could have argued with Durvasa, saying, "Why should I smear this *kheer* all over my body? If you don't like it, throw it into the garbage!" That would be the modern approach! But He did not do so.

Everyone is joyous when things are pleasant, but life is not always filled with pleasant things. What do you do when unpleasant things come? In unpleasant situations, let not your reason be agitated. Rather, understand that unpleasantness caused by people or situations is a test, a gift of God, and if you handle it well you develop willpower. With that awareness of inner will, to your surprise you realize that things that seemed negative are actually positive. Things that were as if destroyed will come to life again; they will be revived.

Those situations in which your expectations are crushed and your feelings are thwarted have their purpose and profound meaning. It is during those experiences that you discover your roots in God. Comfortable situations cannot allow you to rise beyond your ego. If happy situations abounded in human life, you would never turn your mind to God.

As Saint Kabira said, "Of what use is that happiness that takes one's mind away from God? Let that happiness be hanged. Better it is to have pain and misery that directs one's mind to God."

Thus the subtle meaning of worshipping Durvasa in daily life implies developing persistence, endurance and patience, the spirit of forgiving those who hurt you—no matter how many times you are hurt. Remember always that you are not practising patience towards individuals; you are practising patience towards God Who is putting you to test. Krishna was fully aware of this and you can be too. To the extent that you can welcome Durvasa, to that extent you become as Divine as Krishna.

The great secret of spiritual progress, of a life that triumphs over all obstacles, is to able to welcome Durvasa, to be able to serve him at any time, at any cost, sacrificing anything. Then as a result of all this, the grace of Durvasa comes. You discover you have never lost anything in your austerity. Rather, you discover that you have become wealthier and more prosperous. Your wealth becomes the wealth of spirit, the wealth of knowledge, and you discover your essential nature, your unity with God.

Viewed from still another spiritual perspective, Durvasa is a manifestation of Lord Shiva, who is none other than God or the Divine Self. God has two aspects: God the destroyer and God the benevolent. The Shiva concept embraces both. He is God the benevolent, and in that context he is known as Shiva—the embodiment of auspiciousness, the giver of boons, the fulfiller of desires, ever gracious, the personification of compassion. God, however, has another aspect that operates in human life—the aspect that thwarts your desires, that crushes you expectations, that makes you age and destroys the elegance, beauty and health of your body. That aspect is called Rudra the terrible.

To the human mind the Rudra aspect seems terrifying and the gentle Shiva aspect seems most wonderful. When one develops a more mature understanding of life, however, he realizes that both are needed. Good things will not come in your life unless certain things are destroyed. You cannot have a newly designed house unless you demolish the old house. You cannot have a seed sprout unless its old form is destroyed. So construction and destruction must go on side by side. Although destruction fills your heart with a sense of pathos and of cruelty, it heralds the emergence of beauty and glory.

An aspirant must eagerly accept the destruction of egoism, mental impurities, and subtle obstacles that do not allow him to realize the Self. However, while Rudra goes on destroying the illusions that your egoistic attitudes create, your healthier aspirations—those desires that are in harmony with your evolution—are immediately fulfilled by the grace of Lord Shiva. God is the fulfiller of your wishes as well as the destroyer of your illusions. So you view Him in both ways: as the destroyer, the terrible, and the benevolent or most auspicious. That is the beauty of this figurative way of worshiping God as Shiva in both His aspects.

It is that Shiva who appeared in Dwaraka as Durvasa. Though he did a lot of harm to Krishna in the palace, Krishna knew him to be Shiva and maintained a serene mind, considering it a privilege that Shiva was attending on him.

When most people encounter adversity after adversity, they develop a sense of humiliation. But if you possess a spiritual philosophy, instead you develop a sense of pride that God is more interested in you than in others. Lord Shiva is more interested in you because he is after you, shaking you free of all your illusions.

When you wash clothes in the old style the piece of cloth is struck down on a rock again and again. That cloth may shriek and cry out in anger, "How dare you treat me in this rude manner!" But after that ill-treatment the cloth comes forth shining bright. Similarly, when you are beset by apparent adversities, instead of developing a degraded attitude, understand that God is simply being gracious to you! When He inflicts pain He does so out of concern for you—because through pain you are being led to a change that is necessary for your evolution and eventual attainment of Self-realization.

Everyone Is a Part of Yourself

Nothing should be more hated by an aspirant than the negative quality of hatred, and nothing should make him more angry than anger itself. For as long as these vices exist, one is blocked from perceiving and experiencing the glorious nonduality of the Self. The following account of an event at the ashram of Sri Ramana Maharshi in South India expresses this point quite profoundly:

Once several thieves entered the *ashram* of Sri Ramana Maharshi in South India during the night. They thought that since many people visited the Maharshi daily, the *ashram* would have lots of money and costly objects. But to their disappointment they could not find anything. At that time the Maharshi was absorbed in deep meditation. The thieves asked the Maharshi for his wealth, and getting no response from him, they struck him with a stick. Some disciples woke up because of the noise and commotion. They rushed to Ramana Maharshi and saw what had happened. By that time the thieves had taken to their heels.

Angry about the injuries inflicted upon their Guru, the disciples took sticks in their hands crying out, "We are going to take care of those miscreants!" Sri Ramana Maharshi said, "Do not go after them. Stop and think. If your teeth bite your tongue, do you knock them off?" In reflecting on that question, the disciples learned a profound spiritual lesson.

You would never think of knocking out your teeth if they bite your tongue because both teeth and tongue are part of one existence. You simply continue taking your teeth to the dentist to be cared for and pampered.

Similarly, you are related to all the people and beings around you just as your teeth are related to your tongue, or your hands are related to your feet. In other words, all beings are integrally related to the Cosmic Whole, all are part of the same Self. That was the lesson Ramana Maharshi wanted his disciples to understand, and that stirring vision of the Nonduality of the Self is the goal of all spiritual movement.

GREED
(LOBHA)

In *Srimad Bhagavad Gita*, *kama*, *krodha*, and *lobha* are referred to as the triple gates to hell. In the previous chapters we have started to close the first two gates! Now the third gate—*lobha* or greed—is awaiting our attention. If it is not closed, there is no security for the human personality.

Due to ignorance (*avidya*) and inadequte philosophical insight, the minds of most people abound with innumerable desires. The constant pressure exerted by these desires weakens the will and causes that all-devouring, gluttonous demon of greed to thrive in human personality.

Greed and craving are, figuratively speaking, an insult to all that is Divine. One suffering from the disease of *lobha* defiles Divinity and drives Divine grace away from his heart. This is well-illustrated in the following story about a misguided devotee:

The Sooty Buddha

In Tibet there is a temple with a thousand Buddhas, and a devotee selected one of the many Buddhas for his worship. Every day he would bring some costly incense and a ghee-fed lamp and place it before his chosen Buddha. However, he observed that the fragrance of his incense would drift towards the other Buddhas and this upset him. What he bought was very costly and he felt it should all be for his own Buddha and not anyone else's.

As he pondered the situation with great frustration, he came up with an idea to prevent the fragrance from going to the other Buddhas. He was a bit of a carpenter, so he brought some wooden boards and created a wall all around his Buddha.

Now he started burning his candle and incense and was very pleased to see every bit of the fragrance and light that he offered going right to his own Buddha. However, within a week, much to his dismay, his Buddha became black due to all the smoke that was confined within the walls of his shrine.

If you are the kind of person who wants all happiness in life for yourself and none for others, you are like that man striving not to let any fragrance go to any of the other Buddhas. Walling yourself in with "me and mine" constricts your soul and limits your happiness. The Buddha, or the spirit within you, becomes sooty with selfishness. When you turn within yourself, you find no happiness, just sorrow.

On the other hand, if you adopt a process of activity which opens your heart and frees the soul instead of constricting it, you will find that when you turn within, the Buddha within your heart shines bright and your spirit is joyous.

Craving Never Ages

Bhartrihari says, *"Trishnaa na jeernaa, vayameva jeerna,"* which means, "Craving does not age; it does not decay, but we ourselves continue to age." In fact, as a human being ages, his craving seems to become more and more youthful. This understanding is well-illustrated by the following story about an aging king:

Once in ancient times there lived King Yayati, who, like others of his day, had lived a long, long time. One day Yayati noticed old age coming, and although he had enjoyed the sensuous pleasures of life intensely during his life, he suddenly became worried that now he would be devoid of pleasures. He saw a dark future brooding over him and was overcome by despair.

However, it so happened that a sage had given him a boon because of some good karma performed years before. That special boon gave him the power to exchange ages with any younger person willing to do so.

Remembering that boon, King Yayati asked his young children if any one of them would take his age in exchange for their youth. One of his children, who possessed great dispassion towards the pleasures of life even at a tender age, replied, "O Father, I will be glad to exchange my youth for your age." And so the exchange was made and Yayati became young again, and again he lived a life of intense pleasure.

But time passed on as it must and King Yayati again found his body aging. However, his craving for pleasure was still as strong as ever! Thus he realized the impossibility of ever satisfying one's worldly desires by merely having more and more experiences. Finally filled with *vairagya* (dispassion), he composed the following poem.

"Craving is like fire, and enjoyments of the senses are like oblations of *ghee* (clarified butter) poured into the fire, making it blaze higher and higher. Who could ever quench fire by feeding its flame? The urge for pleasure cannot be fulfilled by all the pleasures of the world."

As the story aptly conveys, one who pursues a quantitative concept of pleasure will never be satisfied. He simply continues to hanker for more and more, yet is never fulfilled. Greed is described as a wolf—yet it is even hungrier than a wolf. Even a wolf has a limited stomach, but greed has no limitation.

The interrelation of Desire, Anger, Greed and Delusion

In Chapter Two of *Srimad Bhagavad Gita*, verses 62 and 63, Lord Krishna suggests the powerful interrelation of *kama* (desire), *krodha* (anger), *lobha* (greed) and *moha* (delusion).

"By constantly dwelling upon objects, one develops attachment to them. From attachment there arises desire. From desire there is born anger."

"From anger there arises delusion, from delusion loss of memory. From loss of memory one loses the function of pure reason, and from loss of reason one heads towards destruction."

As these verses suggest, a degrading chain of events, which is all too common in human life, commences with a simple thought about an object (in Vedantic terms, "objects" refer to persons and other living creatures as well as inanimate objects) that promises some form of happiness. At first you merely take a fleeting fancy to the object; then day after day you reinforce that fancy by thinking about the object again and again. Soon your mind develops a psychological leaning or inner attachment—called *sanga*—towards that object. When there is *sanga*, your reasoning begins to be affected and you feel that you cannot live without the object. Thus the desire—*kama*—to possess the object becomes established within your mind. From that desire anger is born.

"Anger" in this particular context has a special interpretation. It means agitation in the mind. When there is desire, two things may happen. You may have fulfillment of the desire, or frustration of the desire. In both cases there is agitation.

When there is fulfillment of a desire, agitation first takes the form of elation. A person becomes elated because anything that is unreal—such as the deluded understanding that objects are the source of happiness—cannot settle in your mind in a natural way. It always creates a reaction.

That is why when people become suddenly prosperous or successful, they often don't know how to handle it. Immediately, they must have a drinking party with feverish antics to handle the elation. In broad terms, that elated agitation is also a form of *krodha*.

Further, if a desire is fulfilled it does not die away. Rather, it usually leads to greed or *lobha*. Why should a person become greedy if his desire is fulfilled? Shouldn't he be happy that he desired something and now he's attained it? Unfortunately, whenever a desire is fulfilled, the mind begins to use simple mathematics: "If I received an ounce of happiness from this object today, I will have more and more happiness from it the longer I cling to it. If this one object has yielded one ounce of happiness, then a hundred objects will yield a hundred ounces. If I have succeeded in acquiring one type of pleasure, why shouldn't I succeed in acquiring other pleasures?"

The agitated mind fails to realize that happiness is not quantitative. You cannot gather an ounce of happiness here, and an ounce there, and thus accumulate a storehouse of happiness. Happiness, in fact, is qualitative.

Thus if desire is fulfilled, there can develop two forms of agitation: the initial elation of getting what you wanted, and the all-consuming greed that ensues because you want more and more of it.

If desire is unfulfilled or frustrated, the agitation of anger develops. You immediately want to blame someone or something for keeping you from having what you desire. As your frustrated desires become suppressed, the agitation of craving, or *trishna*, invades the mind. If you didn't satisfy some desire, then your imagination convinces you how much you are suffering because of this lack. Thus, the desire becomes craving.

So, *kama, krodha* and *lobha* —desire, anger and greed—are intimately related. Further, the mind that is invaded by these demoniac qualities becomes afflicted with delusion and loss of pure reason, and easily follows a degrading and self-destructive course of action which yields nothing but misery and despair. This truth is well-illustrated by the following story from the Middle East.

The Merchant Who Was Blinded by Greed

There was once a merchant in the Middle East who had many camels — animals which used to be the sole mode of transportation in desert lands. Just as nowadays people rent cars, in ancient times people rented camels! So, whenever travelers wanted to do some business in the desert, this merchant would rent them as many camels as they needed.

One day an ascetic who possessed mystical powers came to the merchant and said, "I need many camels and your assistance for a special project that will make you rich. Would you like to help me?"

"Of course," replied the merchant. "What type of assistance do you need?"

"I have come to know about a great treasure of precious jewels, gold and silver and I will need your help to dig it up and thirty camels to carry it. As payment, I will give you one camel load of treasure as your very own. This will make you so rich that you will not have to work anymore for the rest of your life."

The merchant accepted the offer eagerly and they set out across the desert. With the help of the ascetic's special psychic powers, they located the exact spot where the treasure was buried and dug up many treasure chests full of diamonds, rubies, emeralds, gold, and silver, which they loaded on the thirty camels. They then prepared to depart.

The merchant was thrilled beyond words with his one-camel-load share of the treasure. Never had he seen precious stones and metals in such abundance, and he hurried homewards to secure his wealth. But on the way he thought, "That ascetic is getting almost áll the treasure, and he's just a mendicant. He doesn't have a wife and children as I do. What is he going to do with all that treasure?"

So he went back to the ascetic, who was leading the other camels laden with jewels, and said, "You are a mendicant, a man of God. What are you going to do with all this treasure?"

The ascetic, partly because of his wisdom and partly because of his common sense in realizing that he was all alone and that the merchant was much stronger, responded, "You are right, I don't need so much. You can have nine more camel-loads if you like."

Eagerly, the merchant took the additional camels laden with treasure and set out again for home. After a little while, though, he began to think, "Wouldn't it be better to take more of the treasure? After all, the ascetic is a man of renunciation. Such a treasure will just distract his mind from his prayers and austerities!"

So he turned back once again and said, "Why should you get so much treasure? If you take so much, your mind will become distracted and you won't devote your time to meditation; you may even fall from the spiritual path. I think that it would be better for both of us if we divided the treasure fifty-fifty."

Trying to appease the merchant's increasing greed, the ascetic answered, "That's all right with me. Go ahead and take what you have asked for."

So the merchant loaded up the additional treasure and departed. But then again he thought to himself, "Why should I leave any of the treasure with him? As a mendicant, he doesn't know how to manage money. I'm a merchant and I will know how to handle it in a much better way. I'll be doing him a big favor by freeing him from the pressure of these material responsibilities."

So the greedy merchant went back again and said to the ascetic, "Why do you need more than one camel-load of this treasure? It will only be a burden to you in every respect."

"All right," responded the ascetic. "Take everything but one load and go on your way."

So the merchant departed again and then was again overcome by his greed for that last camel-load. Hurrying back to the ascetic, he said, "With your psychic powers you can find treasure buried under the earth any time you want! For all the work I have done I should have the rest of the jewels for myself."

"Fine," the ascetic said, sensing that the merchant's greedy desires would drive him to beat him up if he didn't agree to his demands. "Take it all. I'll just keep this little box that we found along with the treasure. The ointment inside will be enough for me."

While the merchant was preparing again to depart, his mind wouldn't let him rest: "That mendicant let me have the entire treasure with no hesitation, yet he clings to that box. There must be some secret in it. I've got to go back and find out what's so special about that box." So he went back to the man again and asked, "Please tell me what's in that box. What secret does it hold?"

"It's a magic ointment. If you apply a drop of it to one of your eyes, you will be able to see all the buried treasure anywhere in the world; then you'll be able to recover however much you want."

"Please apply a drop to my eye and let me see for myself. I want to see if this ointment really works."

So the ascetic applied one drop to his eye and immediately the merchant saw treasures everywhere, wherever they were buried. He was ecstatic. "This is fantastic! Please apply the ointment to the other eye also."

But the ascetic refused. "No, the virtue of the ointment is that if it is applied to one eye, it will reveal all the treasures; if it is applied to both eyes, it will make a person blind."

The merchant wouldn't hear of this. He was positive that the ascetic was hiding some secret. He reasoned that if one drop in one eye gave so much, think of what another drop in the other eye would give. He insisted and pleaded with the mendicant. Finally the mendicant relented. "Very well, I shall apply the ointment to the other eye, but understand that I do so at your own risk. I have already warned you what will happen."

The moment he applied it to his other eye, the merchant became stone-blind. The ascetic laughed, packed up all the treasure that had been the merchant's, and rode off, leaving him blind and miserable.

The merchant lived the rest of his days in a pathetic and frustrated condition because the only way he could make a living was through begging. When people came to give him alms, he would say, "I shall accept your gift if you will box my ears first; then you can give me whatever you like." This entreaty appealed to many crude people who took great delight in slapping and hitting him.

One day the king of the country came to him in disguise. He thought that the phenomenon of a blind beggar asking to be beaten before taking alms was very strange; so he brought him to the royal court and asked him, "Why do you ask for such gross treatment from people? I will not tolerate it; it is uncultured." Then the poor man told the king the story of how he had brought such misery upon himself through his uncontrolled desire and greed. Hearing the sad tale, the king understood and, of course, granted him royal favor that made his life easier.

This story presents an exaggerated—but quite true—description of greed. Just like the merchant in the story, every soul in the world process wants to have objects of enjoyment. If this natural need is kept under control by a proper understanding of life and its goals, it does not lead to problems. Unfortunately, however, the human mind tends to be forever discontented with whatever it has in the world, and greedily desires more and more.

The idea that you will become more comfortable, more relaxed, and more fulfilled by acquiring more and more possessions, fame or power is based upon illusion. No one finds peace and contentment by having more of anything — except philosophical understanding!

Nothing can bring you true contentment except the philosophical understanding that an all-knowing God has provided for you all the important ingredients for your evolution. Every day, at every moment, the Divine Computer has worked out the exact situations that must be presented before you and the resources to deal with them effectively—resources such as your body, your mind, your intellect, the people around you, and all your circumstances.

In order to be truly prosperous you must have a good internal disposition: a mind that can relax, an intellect that can reflect, a heart that can turn to God. If that type of internal wealth is there, then you are truly prosperous; but if you have only outer prosperity and internally you are hollow, then your prosperity is a kind of joke played by Nature.

In order to curb greed and promote true contentment, you have to understand philosophically that the purpose of human life is to attain enlightenment, or God-Realization. You can enjoy objects of the world, but, as the story of the blinded merchant suggests, you should not have both your eyes directed toward them!

One of your eyes should be kept towards God, the other towards the world. The eye that is directed towards God is your intuitive intellect. If you have intuitive intellect, then you have an eye that is intact.

The world-process is like the ointment: you never apply it to both your eyes — the physical as well as the mystical. You have to keep the mystical eye open. If you apply the ointment of the world-process to the mystical eye, too—if you allow your intellect to be colored by the world—then you go stone-blind. All your achievements become nothing. But if you keep your intellect intact by not letting the world touch it, then you enjoy the world. That is, although you live in the world, you have a sense of detachment and freedom that lets you know that you are above the world.

The ascetic was a spiritual teacher who tried to give the merchant this understanding. But the merchant wasn't ready, so he succumbed to inordinate greed and had both eyes blinded.

As the fate of the merchant indicates, every desire that you go after with intense greed will box your ears! Some twist or painful experience is always implied in the fulfillment of uncontrolled desires.

Like the blind man, the soul that is deprived of the mystical vision of the Self experiences degradation. Led by greed, the soul is unable to discover its unity with the Absolute. But when the flame of greed and craving is extinguished, you possess double consciousness: an internal, intuitive vision that "I am one with God," and an external, pragmatic vision that allows you to live with practical reality.

Even though you live in the world, you possess a dimension to your personality that allows you to see beyond it. Not to become totally immersed in the world is the great secret behind all religion and spiritual philosophy. Everyone is led by a process that forces him to be in the world. Everyone is compelled to do certain things, to undertake certain projects, to discover certain talents, to achieve certain things in the world. But if you lose sight of the inner self as you do all these, then all your achievements become nothing, and you end up feeling humiliated—like the blind man who had lost all the treasure.

On the other hand, if you discover that transcendental dimension within yourself, you will perform your duties with purity of mind, and you will not embark upon a project because of uncultured desires, egoism and pride. The work you do will bring about harmony and peace, and it will be auspicious for humanity. The quality of your work will be spiritual; it will carry a heavenly fragrance.

In addition, you will develop an awareness that you are not the doer, that you are ever free. Even though you might be working hard to accomplish things in the course of your daily life, inwardly you will feel that you are ever free and untouched. Even if the greatest calamity were to befall you, it wouldn't shake you. Storm clouds gather, thunder rumbles, lightning flashes, but the sky remains unaffected. Like the sky you are ever untouched.

If that vision were to enter your heart and linger there, your life would be extermely joyous. Referring to the parable, it would be like getting the entire treasure and the box of ointment at the same time and yet keeping one eye safe. But if you do not keep one eye safe — the inner spiritual eye — you wander in a land of illusion, groping in darkness, tumbling from embodiment to embodiment.

The Folly of Comparing Yourself to Others

A greedy person is not aware of his own resources. He is only aware of what others have, and always thinks that others are better off than he is. He becomes like a "dog in the manger." A dog sees food in front of other dogs and thinks that that food is much better than his. As a result, he goes on barking instead of enjoying what he has.

The following adaptation of an ancient story illustrates this point quite graphically:

Once a man practised a lot of austerity. As a result, his Deity came before him saying, "Ask any boon and you shall have it." The man replied, "May I be rich and prosperous." Hearing that, the Deity (who wanted the devotee to gain spiritual under-standing as well as material wealth) said, "Everything that you ask will be given to you—but in addition, your neighbors, in a one block radius from your home, will get double of whatever you get."

At first the man could not understand the impli-cations of his Deity's words and he was quite pleased with his good fortune. He went to his home, an ordinary home, and said, "Let there be a mansion with a nice roof." Immediately everything became as he requested and he admired his mansion with amazement. Then he looked out the window and saw that his neighbors had double-story mansions.

Then he said, "Let there be a beautiful garden blooming around this house." So it happened, but the neighbors got flourishing gardens twice the size of his all around their houses.

As a result of his neighbors' double prosperity, the man's heart began to burn with jealousy every time he asked for something. Finally, his mind be-came so upset that he came up with a diabolical plan. First he willed, "Let there be a well in front of my house." Of course, the others got two wells. Then he said, "Let me be only one-eyed!" His scheme was that by his wishing to become blind in one eye, all his neighbors would become blind in both and readily fall into the two wells that adorned their property. However, that boon was not granted by the Deity. Rather, to teach the greedy and jealous devotee a spiritual lesson, he was left with one eye and a well, while the neighbors all had two eyes and two wells and everything flourishing around them.

As the story reveals, there is so much illusion involved in trying to secure happiness through wealth. A greedy person is always comparing himself to others, and what he has gained is never enough.

A millionaire is very happy until he meets a billionaire, then he feels like a little rabbit before him. Since there are always people who surpass you in some way or the other in wealth, health, looks, power, or fame, the human heart can always be discontented.

Thus, Yoga teaches the importance of not comparing yourself with others. Everyone has been given the best situations for his advancement and is unique. What you have been given no one else possesses in exactly the same way.

Asteya and Aparigraha—
Nonstealing and Noncovetousness

In Raja Yoga, *asteya* and *aparigraha* are two of the five great *yamas* or ethical restraints. *Asteya* implies freedom from desiring, misappropriating or stealing the possessions of others, and *aparigraha* is noncovetousness. In the Old Testament of the Bible, these appear as the eighth and the last of the great Ten Commandments—Thou shalt not steal, Thou shalt not covet. *Asteya* and *aparigraha*—nonstealing and noncovetousness—are closely related sister virtues which are both directed towards the removal of greed.

The Psychological Basis

The urge to steal results from a blend of greed, selfishness, and lack of control over the senses. Afflicted with the illusion that happiness comes from objects, one can be overwhelmed by the urge to get for himself those things which seem to be giving happiness to others.

A thief steals because he feels that he cannot be happy without the objects he craves and his mind lacks the patience to earn them in a righteous way. His mind may at first tell him, "You can get those things by working for them," but then his mind quickly changes its perspective and says, "Why should you work? Why not just enter into a crowd and 'pick a pocket or two!' Or you can just sneak into a house,

showing a little gun and a masked face, and get what
you want. Who is going to catch you?"

The greedy mind does not see the darker implications of that action. It does not see who will get
hurt or what others will feel if they have lost things
which they have loved or worked hard for. Due to
intense selfishness, the mind behaves like a de-
praved vulture and promotes indulgence in falsehood.

If a person is dominated by a highly intense and
perverted form of greed, he chooses this path of
steya, or stealing. On the other hand, if the greed is
more moderate, a person tends toward *parigraha*, or
covetousness. Adopting methods that are normally
considered righteous, he continues to crave objects
and accumulates more and more of them, hoarding
them beyond his needs. Such a person is not stealing
from others, nor misappropriating what they already possess. He simply is obsessed with the idea, "If
I have more and more I will be happier."

Afflicted by covetousness, you strive incessantly
to multiply your possessions. Instead of having two
pairs of shoes, you have fifty pairs; instead of having
a few sweaters, you have a hundred sweaters! As a
result, all year long you have to watch over your
things to see that they don't get mildewed or moth-
eaten!

Afraid to lose all the possessions that you have
acquired, you become tied to a place, tied to objects.
You are a constant caretaker of things that you are

not going to use — things which simply become a source of endless headache for you!

Further, there is a great illusion involved in the idea that by acquiring more and more possessions you will become secure and comfortable. It is like chasing a mirage in order to quench your thirst.

If you were to study your life and the lives of people around you, you would realize that "more" doesn't necessarily mean "happier." A person who is poor thinks that if only he had sufficient money in his hands, he would be happy. But the moment he becomes richer, he wants to have more and more and never feels contented. Normally, as wealth increases, discontent increases in direct proportion — unless you have developed spiritual insight.

Effects of Covetousness on Society

From the social point of view, a person who develops covetousness disturbs the harmony and economic balance of society. Why should one person hoard so many more things than he can use, when those things could have been utilized by others? It is unethical that many are deprived of the conveniences of life while others hoard far beyond any reasonable need. Such hoarding negates the fact that the same life flows in all. It is a form of violence. You are hurting others by developing exaggerated greed, and causing disbalance and disharmony in society.

On the other hand, if people were infused with the virtue of noncovetousness, the ideal would be simple living and high thinking. The ideal would be to go after the greater treasures of life—the spiritual values—and then material wealth will become subservient to spiritual wealth.

In a more cultured and elevated society, there would be an entirely different kind of greed—greed for the attainment of spiritual virtues. One would crave for more and more sincerity, more mental peace, more goodness, more gentleness, more control of mind. People would be extremely discontented with their psychological and spiritual limitations, and hanker to become better and better every day!

If this ideal were practised, there would be peace in the individual who practises it, and he would radiate and promote happiness and peace in the environment around him. This would lead to a higher level of culture for the individual and for society.

The Secret of True Prosperity
When you are greedy, your will becomes weak. As a result of this weakness, you may not be able to get the very objects that you greedily desire. Or if you do get them, they will become a source of pain.

There is a strange law operating in the Divine plan: If you do not deserve an object towards which you have developed greed, that object will repel you. Even if you succeed in possessing it, that object will be painful because it will create many mental complexes.

Thus, you will not really be happy if you get an object because of greed. On the other hand, if you do not have greed, then all the objects that you need in your spiritual evolution will come to you automatically. An interesting parable is told to illustrate this point:

A devotee was practising meditation and had a strange vision when he invoked Goddess Lakshmi — the Goddess of Prosperity. The Goddess, whom he expected to appear before him in a luminous and radiant form, appeared with Her forehead badly bruised and Her feet terribly sore. The devotee, seeing Lakshmi Devi in this strange condition, asked, "Oh Goddess, how is this possible? How can you, who are the giver of prosperity to all, have your forehead bruised and your feet swollen and sore?"

The Goddess replied, "Oh devotee, I will answer your question and reveal to you a great secret. There are so many worldly-minded people who crave for Me and pursue Me, and yet do not deserve Me. And I have to go on kicking them from morning till night. Imagine how much my feet hurt because I must go on doing that day after day!

"And then there are some rare souls who have truly renounced greed and who tread the path of spirituality. They are so dispassionate that they don't want Me at all. In the Divine Plan, however, they must have some of My wealth in order to help mankind. So I go to their doors and, adopting the Eastern method, I repeatedly bow and strike my head against the thresholds in order to persuade them to accept Me. This goes on day after day, so that now My forehead has become terribly bruised!"

The parable shows that if you are devoid of greed, you attract the Goddess of Prosperity, Who wants to bestow Her blessings. On the other hand if you go after objects through greed, then the Goddess of Prosperity goes on kicking you, as it were. Crave wealth and wealth will renounce you. Renounce craving, and all the wealth of the world will pursue you.

A person who is free from greed is able to command matter and all material needs. He is the master of matter and uses matter according to his need. But when the mind is weakened by greed, one allows himself to be used by matter. If you are the master of your possessions, you are prosperous. If the possessions are possessing you, then you are not prosperous.

If you perform your self-effort in the world without being attached to material prosperity, you will draw prosperity by commanding it. Nature will give you everything that you deserve. In a mysterious way, what you need will come to you, and you will be able to use your prosperity well.

On the other hand, if you draw wealth out of greed, that wealth will make you fearful because you will always be afraid of losing it. Further, you will want to assert that you are wealthy, and that will make you conceited and arrogant. If worldly prosperity comes to you when you are psychologically dependent on the world, it results in tremendous illusion, and makes you insensitive. In this case, it is more a curse than a boon.

External or material prosperity is not healthy unless it is accompanied by internal prosperity. Unless your material success is accompanied by the development of Divine qualities within your personality, it is not healthy prosperity. People can become externally rich without having any inner wealth at all. When this happens, they are certainly not prosperous in any real sense.

If you burden a donkey with sandalwood, the donkey doesn't enjoy the sandalwood. It becomes only a load to carry. Similarly, if a lot of wealth comes to a greedy person who has no cultured idea of what to do with it, that wealth is just like a lot of sandalwood on a donkey's back.

All that most wealthy people feel during their life is the pressure of their wealth, the burden. And carrying that burden they depart — leaving the load they had carried to be used by somebody else. Can that be called prosperity?

The Fruit of Asteya and Aparigrahaa

If one is free of greed and truly established in non-stealing, he has discovered the secret of abundance. Raja Yoga says, *"Asteya Pratisht-hayam Sarva Ratnopasthanam"*—"When a person is established in nonstealing, he acquires the power of attracting all jewels and pearls—all wealth—to himself."

All the wealth of the physical, psychological and spiritual world flows to one who is imbued with the true spirit of renunciation. He becomes blessed with true contentment, peace and harmony. The practice of *asteya* opens his heart to the abundance of Divine consciousness and leads him to the treasure of treasures: Self-realization!

Similarly, if you stopped chasing after things beyond your need, what would happen? Raja Yoga says, *"Aparigraha-sthairye janma kathanta sambodhah."*—"By attaining perfection in noncovetousness, one acquires the knowledge of past births."

If you were to root out the subtle seeds of greed from your unconscious and unburden your mind of *parigraha* (covetousness), then that mind would reveal to you that you are a spirit—a traveler who has moved again and again from one embodiment to another—and you would have a clear memory of your past lives.

But under the pressure of attachment to possessions and strong identification with your body, you can't remember this great fact. Tied down to your body and its possessions, that subtle instinctive sense that brings to you the memories of past lives is obscured.

That special power of the mind to remember the past incarnations is veiled by your present attachments. Because you become so attached to the objects around you, you cannot imagine that in other lives you were completely detached from them and had nothing to do with them. Your mind becomes so entangled by the realities that have evolved in this present personality that you are unable to imagine that you previously had different personalities, and in each personality you had different relationships and realities around you.

The moment greed is eliminated and the mind relaxes, you begin to develop the awareness, "I am a spirit and this world is not my final stay. I am in transit. As a personality I exist in this world for only a short time." When you fly in a plane, you exist in the plane for only a limited time. Then the plane must land and you must walk out to go to your destination. Similarly, in all your embodiments you are in transit, and you must walk out of those embodiments to attain liberation, to enter into *Brahman*—the ultimate destination of every soul.

So, the practice of noncovetousness first brings forth that hidden insight into the nature of your spirit and the manner in which it moves from one embodiment to another through karma. You understand that the realities to which you become attached come and go like waves in the ocean of millions of embodiments and, like waves, they will pass on without affecting you. You will continue to incarnate, led by your karma.

With further purity of mind you understand that your innermost spirit is not an individualized entity. The real nature of your spirit is the Self—the Universal Spirit. When you realize intuitively, from the depths of your being, "I am That, I am the Absolute Self," you attain liberation and the process of reincarnation terminates.

PRIDE
(MADA)

As an aspirant you must have a certain *satwic* pride in yourself in order to succeed in *sadhana* (spiritual discipline) and handle your practical realities effectively. You should be proud of being born in a human embodiment, proud of following the path of Yoga, proud that you have the inner resources to progress on the spiritual path leading to Liberation. These forms of pride are *satwic* and of value in the process of evolution.

However, there are *rajasic-tamasic* forms of pride—known as *mada*—which must be quelled day by day with great zeal. Egoism, conceit, vanity, arrogance, insolence, obstinacy, cruelty and selfishness—all these form the family of *mada* and its relatives.

The Sanskrit word *mada* is quite similar to the Sanskrit word *madira*, which means intoxicating liquor. People under the influence of intoxicating liquor lose their mental balance and their power of reasoning. So too, pride makes your mind so intoxicated that you don't know who you are, what is your goal, what is right and what is wrong.

The Ego of King Akbar

King Akbar, a great king in India during the sixteenth century, had a very witty minister named Birbal. Birbal had many enemies among the court officers because he was always favored by the king.

One day these officers thought up a plan to degrade Birbal. They started spreading the idea that the King was like God. They knew that Birbal would not agree to that, and if Birbal did not agree to it, the king would punish him. Certainly every king wants to be praised, and could not bear anyone who would not praise him.

So the officers started bowing to the King saying, "Oh King, to us you are God himself. But Birbal doesn't hold that view." King Akbar, who was very pleased with this praise, looked at Birbal and said, "How is it that you do not agree with what the officers are saying? Don't you have any reverence for me?" Birbal replied, "Why should I agree with these people? I consider you greater than God."

"How so?" King Akbar asked, intrigued by this response. Birbal replied, "If someone commits an error, God cannot drive him out of His kingdom, because His kingdom includes the entire universe. However, if someone commits an error in your kingdom, you have the power to drive him out. Therefore, you are above God."

The subtle implication of this story is that when you have ego, you place yourself above God. The things around you are controlled by God's plan. But ego becomes overly assertive and makes you feel as if you are moving the world.

The Pride of
Kakabhushundi

In the Tulasi *Ramayana*, there is an interesting story—told by Kakabhushundi to Garuda—of how he had become a crow and why he had chosen to remain in that embodiment through all cycles of creation:

In one of his previous incarnations, Kakabhushundi was a young, arrogant devotee of Shiva. Even though his guru again and again instructed him not to hate Vishnu and the worshipers of Vishnu, Kakabhushundi continued to do so. He even began to hate the guru himself for asking him to be broad-minded, and became insulting to the guru in various ways.

One day, Kakabhushundi was seated in the temple offering prayers to Shiva when the guru entered the temple. Out of arrogance, Kakabhushundi stayed seated and did not rise to welcome him. Suddenly the voice of Shiva rang out in the temple and cursed Kakabhushundi, saying, "Oh ungrateful disciple, since you have stayed seated like a snake, may you become a snake and continue to incarnate through thousands of embodiments as lower forms of life."

Hearing this curse from Shiva, Kakabhushundi trembled, and the guru was moved by profound compassion for him. The guru then prayed to Shiva to withdraw the curse He had imposed. Appeased by the heartfelt prayer, Shiva reduced the curse by ordaining that those lower embodiments would pass very quickly. Further, He told the disciple, "After exhausting your thousand embodiments, you will be born in Ayodhya, the sacred city of Rama. And there, by My grace and by the force of *satsanga*, devotion to Rama will arise in your heart. But remember, never again should you displease a spiritual preceptor. Consider all saints and sages as *Brahman* himself."

According to the words of Shiva, the disciple was eventually born into a *brahmin* family in Ayodhya and, from his very childhood, was immersed in worshiping Rama. After his parents died he entered into forest life and approached a sage for spiritual initiation. The sage began to expound the non-dualistic philosophy of *Vedanta*, the path of Jnana Yoga, but the *brahmin* youth was not happy with this teaching. His mind was so intensely devoted to the worship of the personal form of Rama and to the path of Bhakti Yoga that he insisted again and again that he should be given initiation into that path.

Angered by the disciple's stubborn insistence, the sage cursed him, saying, "May you become a crow." The boy accepted that curse lovingly, as if it were a welcome blessing, and immediately began to fly while adoring the sage. Seeing this, the sage regretted having cursed the boy and revealed to him a secret: that he taught Jnana Yoga to most people, but kept Bhakti Yoga for a very select type of highly qualified aspirant. Since the disciple proved to be that type of aspirant, the guru then began to initiate him into the path of devotion, teaching him the art of meditating on Rama as a child through the aspect of devotion known as *vatsalya bhava* (loving God as parents would love their child). The guru further blessed the disciple with the ability to easily understand the hidden secrets of the scriptures and to develop ever-increasing love for Rama. In addition, he would have the power to assume any physical form of his choice.

As a result of those blessings and initiation, the disciple became Sage Kakabhushundi, a great devotee of Rama, and attained oneness with the Absolute. Because of a rare boon received from Rama, he had the power to maintain his body as long as he wished, and so he continues to live on through ages and ages in order to teach others the path of devotion and knowledge. Although he could have assumed any form he wished—including the human form—he retains the beloved crow embodiment in which he attained oneness with Rama. In this form, he continues to hold *satsanga* as numerous birds come and listen to his teachings. Further, whenever Rama incarnates in any age, Kakabhushundi goes to Ayodhya and watches the baby Rama playing and delighting his parents. Then he returns to his Himalayan *ashram* again and resumes his teachings.

This story about how Kakabhushundi had to overcome his arrogance and pride in order to attain enlightenment can be taken literally, as a portrayal of how every soul evolves through many embodiments until spiritual perfection is attained. Or it can be taken as a mystic portrayal of spiritual transformation in general. Even as one evolves spiritually in one lifetime, many changes occur. A person who slithers crookedly like a snake in his youth may experience a dramatic personality change as he grows wiser. He may become simple and innocent like a dove, dynamic like a hawk, elevated and detached like a swan. A swan sports in a lake but it doesn't belong to the lake. The moment the swan desires to fly, it shakes off all the water particles from its feathers and soars. Similarly, in the state of realization, one develops the ability to shake off the world at any time and to soar beyond the world to the realm of transcendence.

The crow has been given a special symbolic significance in Indian scriptures. It is not considered the ugly, lowly creature that many cultures consider it to be. Rather, the crow is considered unique because it is described as possessing only one eye that rolls back and forth between two sockets.

Whether this is biologically true or not doesn't matter. What does matter is that this conception makes the crow a symbol of double consciousness— of a sage's ability to switch his vision between the transcendental and the relative at a moment's notice. At one moment a sage is immersed in the highest reality that transcends all, and at another moment, he comes back to the world, aware of every practical reality.

The emphasis placed in Kakabhushundi's story on not insulting a guru or spiritual preceptor reminds an aspirant of the importance of not developing any negative attitudes that hinder his spiritual advancement. In this context, insulting a spiritual preceptor implies turning away from the path that leads to liberation, which is the greatest injury that one can do to himself, and leads to the greatest loss that one can experience.

The Rise and Fall of the Ego

In *Devi Bhagavata* there is another story that graphically illustrates the degrading nature of pride. It is the story of the rise and fall of the great King Nahusha:

Once there was a great and powerful king in ancient India named Nahusha. During his reign he performed various sacrifices and righteous acts. Because of his meritorious deeds, his ability to enjoy heavenly delights was heightened.

According to the story, Indra, the king of gods, had to go into seclusion for some time and stay away from his normal duties. Immediately there arose the question of who would rule the heavenly world in Indra's absence. The gods and sages therefore convened to choose a successor. In reviewing the possible candidates, they found that King Nahusha of the mortal world had attained great spiritual qualities and undoubtedly deserved to be the ruler of Heaven; so they proposed that Nahusha succeed Indra as ruler.

Immediately a messenger was dispatched to report their decision to King Nahusha. He was told that he was promoted to the heavenly world and that he would become the new Indra—ruler of the gods. Nahusha was highly pleased to hear this news and he entered the heavenly world and began his rulership.

But such exaltation, instead of making him humbler, made him swollen-headed. Formerly he had been a righteous person, but actually his righteousness had not been very profound; ego still dominated his mind to a great extent. Because of this he gradually developed intense pride in his position in the heavenly world. The gods and sages were not pleased with the changes in Nahusha, but since they had chosen him for his position, they allowed him to have his way.

Soon, however, Nahusha's pride grew even more and he began to covet Indra's wife, Indrani Shachi. His mind was constantly obsessed with the thought, "Why shouldn't Shachi become my wife? Just think of the glory and prestige she would bring me."

Presently news was sent to Shachi that she should come and accept Nahusha as her husband. When

Shachi was brought before him, Nahusha said to her, "You shall accept me as your husband, and both of us then will enjoy the heavenly glory. Think no more of your husband who is dead and gone. Even if he is alive he may as well be dead, because he is no longer ruling the heavenly realm."

Shachi tried to persuade Nahusha not to insist on her becoming his wife, but he was adamant and wouldn't hear of it. The more she pleaded the angrier he got. Seeing Nahusha's anger, even the gods and sages were afraid. They did not know what to do about his terrible ego, or how to divest him of the power they had invested in him.

Seeing that Nahusha would not compromise, Shachi asked him for some time to think about his proposal. Nahusha acquiesced. In the meantime Shachi went to Brihaspati, the guru of gods, for shelter and advice. Brihaspati counseled her that the only one who could help her in this situation was Goddess Saraswati; so he initiated her into the worship of the Goddess. Shachi offered adorations to Goddess Saraswati, and the Goddess gave her insight about what to do. With her intellect touched by the grace of Goddess Saraswati, Shachi knew how to handle the situation.

She sent a message to Nahusha saying that she would accept him as her husband, but that he should come to her in a palanquin carried by sages. She expressed her view that every god had a special vehicle: Lord Vishnu rode on Garuda, Shiva on a bull, etc. Since he was a person from the mortal world who rose to such great power, he must have a unique vehicle; therefore, he should be brought to her on a palanquin carried by sages. Surely, no one had ever thought of such a form of transportation!

Nahusha, with his pride and tremendous ego, didn't realize that he was being tricked; rather, he felt that he was being honored. "Surely all the gods

and sages adore me," his message stated. "Whatever I say they will do; so I shall come to you on a palanquin borne by sages."

And Shachi replied, "Very well, my lord, I shall await you."

Soon after this Nahusha chose a group of sages and asked them to bear the palanquin. They told him they would be happy to do it and smiled knowingly among themselves, for they knew what was waiting for Nahusha. Among them was the great Agastya, the most exalted of sages. There were others of great standing also. At the appointed time, the sages picked up the heavenly palanquin and hoisted it upon their shoulders for the journey to Shachi. Nahusha sat upon it, bursting with pride as he eagerly awaited the moment when he would claim Shachi as his wife.

From the outset, however, Nahusha was annoyed with the sages because they weren't able to synchronize their movements and they moved much more slowly than he had expected. He sullenly thought to himself, "Lord Vishnu's vehicle moves a lot faster than mine. Come to think of it, everyone's vehicle moves faster. I made a big mistake to agree to this." In his impatience he scolded the sages, shouting, "*Sarpa, sarpa*—Quick, quick! Move faster!" His choice of words was most significant in this context, because the Sanskrit word, *sarpa*, has a double meaning: it can mean "snake" as well as "quick."

Nahusha's shouts to move faster caused the sages to quicken their pace to the extent that they could. But their outpouring of effort and energy still didn't suit Nahusha. Screaming, "*Sarpa, sarpa!*" at the top of his lungs, the King lost his temper and kicked Agastya in the back as hard as he could. Agastya immediately cursed him: "May you become a *sarpa*—a snake!" So he turned into a snake that instant and fell from Heaven down to the mortal world. There he remained for many centuries as a snake until he met King Yudhishthira at the time of the Mahabharata War.

Though a snake, he was still able to talk like a human being and thus was able to hold many interesting conversations with King Yudhishthira. Because of the contact he had with the great king, who was the embodiment of righteousness, his spirit was liberated; but in spite of this, he still had to go through a long process of suffering and degradation before this happened.

This story symbolically portrays the rise and fall of ego, as represented by Nahusha. When a person performs *sakamya karmas*, or actions prompted by the desire for heavenly enjoyment, the fruit he reaps from doing such actions leads him to heavenly enjoyment. But enjoying that fruit of righteousness is not equivalent to attaining liberation. King Nahusha was a great monarch who performed many good deeds, but as we saw, simply performing good deeds with no philosophical insight does not eliminate ego. And if ego is present, there will always be a basis for degradation.

If you have philosophical insight you do not seek a reward in heaven; you seek the dissolution of ego itself. You perform actions for *chitta shudhi*, or purity of the heart, not for enjoyment on the astral plane.

Another point illustrated by the parable is that if the unconscious has not been purified—if real aspiration has not developed—then possessions, power, and glory all create a twisted intellect. If a person lacking purity of intellect attains great power he becomes swollen-headed. If you cannot handle power you will fall, and that is what happened to Nahusha.

Shachi is the principle of pure intellect, which cannot be owned by ego. Any effort to dominate the intellect by an egoistic process is a movement that will lead one to degradation.

Yoking the sages to a palanquin also has mystical significance. When you have not brought order in your personality, it is like a runaway chariot. The chariot of your personality has to be driven by the higher principles of your soul, such as understanding, reasoning and reflection (symbolized by the sages), not by your ego. But instead, the lesser in you tries to dominate the higher.

The right destination for the ego is that state wherein it is effaced. When ego allows itself to be effaced, there lies its exaltation, its grandeur. But when ego allows itself to be intensified, degradation results. This seems paradoxical, but therein lies the subtle mystery of mysticism: you enjoy existence more when your ego dissolves.

Thus, when Nahusha tried to dominate the sages he initiated his own downfall. Instead of possessing Shachi, his soul fell into a state of degradation and bondage.

Further, the story shows that by adoring Goddess Saraswati you allow your ego to be dominated by pure intellect. By making you reflective, Goddess allows you to have proper reasoning and insight. If you exalt your ego, however, and live for egoistic values—power, fame, glory, and wealth—then the same Goddess who can enlighten the intellect deludes it. This is the same process that caused Nahusha to fall. The Goddess in you is ever ready either to delude your intellect or to enlighten it.

When you turn towards egoistic feelings such as selfishness, greed, and vanity, the Saraswati within you smiles in a sinister way, causing your intellect to become gradually twisted. Though you may think that you are doing good to yourself, you are actually creating a basis for future sorrow. On the other hand, when you follow the path of righteousness and allow good qualities to develop, the Saraswati within you smiles in a heavenly way and your intellect begins to recover its brilliance. You begin to understand the subtle secrets of life and discover the simplest way to transcend all your troubles and turmoils. This is the process by which intellect becomes intuitive. Figuratively speaking, your soul rushes toward the heavenly world. On the other hand, when ego dominates, the soul rushes headlong down into the world-process.

INSIGHT INTO HUMILITY

Humility is a divine virtue which is the positive counterpart of pride or *mada*. It is the expression of an evolving soul—a soul that is winging its way to the Divine Self. Humility implies effacement of ego, and it is attained by an individual in gradual degrees.

When the mind is highly fulfilled, without the pressure of the unconscious *vasanas* (subtle desires), ego is transcended and one begins to experience one's unity with the Divine Self. In that state of perfection, there is an utter absence of ego, a spontaneous blossoming of supreme humility.

The Foot of Sage Bhrigu

In the *Puranas* there is a story that gives insight into the quality of humility in its highest and most perfect form:

Once Gods were having a discussion about Who among the Deities was the greatest: Brahma—the Creator, Vishnu—the Sustainer, or Shiva—the Destroyer?

"Brahma is the greatest because he is the creator of the universe. He is the teacher of the *Vedic* wisdom. Being the embodiment of righteousness, He is the guide and guru of all beings." This was the view upheld by some divine beings.

"Lord Shiva is the greatest because by His immense power He brings about the destruction of the world. If Shiva did not destroy the world, the cycle of creation and dissolution could not be maintained."

Thus some argued for establishing the greatness of Shiva.

"Lord Vishnu is the greatest," asserted the devotees of Lord Vishnu. "He is the sustainer of the world. Creation and destruction are sustained by Him. It is He who incarnated as Rama and Krishna, and it is He who incarnates from time to time to promote harmony and order in the world."

Unsatisfied, however, with these answers, Sage Bhrigu took upon himself the task of finding out who is the greatest among the three Deities. He reflected within himself, "I will consider Him the greatest who is endowed with the greatest degree of forbearance, who has the greatest control over his temper." With this idea in mind, he first proceeded to *Bramha Loka*, the heavenly region where Lord Brahma dwells.

Having entered *Brahma Loka*, he approached Brahma without offering adorations. Brahma could not tolerate this misconduct of the Sage. Anger manifested in His face as the corners of His eyes grew red, and He began to look for His *kamandalu* (the vessel containing sacred water) with the intention of pronouncing a curse on Bhrigu. Goddess Saraswati, the Divine consort of Lord Brahma, restrained him, saying, "O Lord, do not be angry with Bhrigu. He has always been courteous before. There must be some reason for his unusual behavior." Thus saying, Goddess Saraswati dissuaded Brahma from cursing the Sage.

Scarcely believing that he had escaped, Sage Bhrigu hastened his steps to the dwelling place of Lord Shiva. Approaching the great Deity, he did not salute. In addition, he began to insult the Deity, saying, "O Shiva, you ride on a Bull, wear snakes for your garlands, and keep your body besmeared with ashes. You are the very personification of madness!"

At this, Lord Shiva grew immensely angry and reached for his trident, ready to hurl it to destroy Bhrigu. But Goddess Parvati, Lord Shiva's Divine consort, stopped Him, pleading, "O Lord, Bhrigu is a great Sage and devotee of ours. Please have patience with him." Reluctantly Lord Shiva withdrew His trident saying, "This *brahmin* must be taught a lesson. However, I am not beheading him this time for your sake. But if he ever shows rudeness again, his head will fall!"

Fleeing from Lord Shiva, Bhrigu proceeded to Vaikuntha where Lord Vishnu dwells. Lord Vishnu, the indweller of every heart, knew what the Sage was intending to do, and even before Bhrigu arrived, He pretended to be deep in sleep. When Bhrigu arrived at Vaikuntha, he rushed towards the Divine abode. The gate-keepers tried to stop the Sage from entering, but seeing his angry face, they let him go. Bhrigu rushed into the inner apartments of Lord Vishnu, and seeing Him stretched in sleep, the Sage kicked the chest of Lord Vishnu with great vehemence, saying, "You who are the sustainer of the world, how dare you sleep, ignoring the well-being of the world!"

Lord Vishnu sat up and clasped the feet of the Sage, saying, "O Sage, your tender lotus foot has been injured by my rock-like chest. What a great sin I have committed! Please forgive me, O great Sage!"

Sage Bhrigu was amazed at the humility of Lord Vishnu. He said, "O Lord, it is I who must be forgiven by You who are supremely compassionate. How can I ever be free of the sinful act of having kicked Your sacred chest with my foot? The world will always speak ill of me for having done so."

Lord Vishnu said, "O Sage, on the contrary, the world will sing your praises. You have pleased Me by placing your foot on My chest. Just as a mother is pleased even when her infant kicks her, I am ever pleased with My devotees even when they are angry with Me. As a token of My satisfaction, I have installed your footprint on My chest. Not only this, every great incarnation of Mine will bear your footprint on His chest."

Sage Bhrigu was immersed in bliss. He had discovered the greatest among the Deities!

From a mystic point of view, this story is not meant to ascertain the superiority of one Deity over another, because, in fact, these three Deities are One appearing as three. What it intends to do is show the secret of real greatness. The greatness of a person does not lie in his power and prosperity, but in the magnanimity of his heart—the magnanimity with which he is ever ready to love instead of hate, to forgive instead of bear a grudge, to be humble instead of proud and conceited.

The perfect and total humility of Lord Vishnu is Divine, beyond the human plane. As long as one is in the human plane, his interactions are based on ego to one degree or another. But the ideal of egolessness personified in this story must be adored, and one must strive to realize that ideal gradually with patience.

Blessed Are the Meek

"Blessed are the meek, For they shall inherit the earth." This third beatitude from Lord Jesus' Sermon on the Mount extols the great virtue of humility and points to its majestic power. The "meekness" referred to here is profoundly different from the "meekness" of common parlance. It is not to be confused with the dullness of mind that leads a person to simply accept without questioning whatever the world presents before him. Nor is it at all like the degrading timidity that leaves many people feeling humiliated again and again in life. Certainly it is not the feigned humility that a crafty person adopts to help him get what he wants out of a situation. Such a person may act like a sheep, but he may well be a wolf in sheep's clothing!

The blessed meekness praised by Lord Jesus is that Yogic state of advanced personality integration in which one is so profoundly in tune with Cosmic Will that he has no need to assert his ego. Ever guided by the Divine hand, he carries out the will of God with total surrender, with the innocent meekness of a sheep driven by the Great Shepherd—God, the Divine Self.

The highest state of "meekness" is reached when a devotee is able to totally cast his ego-center into the ocean of the Divine Self through the intuitive realization of God. This is achieved through a mind which sees the very ego-center as merely a reflection of that Self, and not the absolute reality within.

In the lesser stages of spiritual development, the ego center seems to be all that one has, and one is constantly trying to assert the ego. However, as you reflect deeply and enquire into "Who am I?," you gradually realize the illusoriness of the perception of ego, and the vanity involved in being a slave to egoistic consciousness. You eventually understand that the ego is not the all-important factor that it appeared to be and the tension due to egoistic illusions gradually begins to subside.

One who has developed such meekness of spirit enjoys a unique type of relaxation and experiences a joy that so far excels ordinary happiness that it is termed as Bliss. His mind is no longer under the grip of selfishness, no longer tarnished by the impressions of frustrations and sorrow that accompany eogistic consciousness. The radiantly healthy mind of such a person becomes a basis for intense creative activity that can do immeasurable good for many, many people.

Mind is a form of Divine energy and it is necessary that an aspirant use that energy with respect. If you use your mental energy properly and see that your mind is kept relaxed and cheerful day by day, then Nature flows through that mind creating wonders. You begin to think powerful thoughts that you would never have imagined possible. You begin to enjoy highly sublime feelings and sentiments. Through that mind you begin to discover what is really meant by universal love and nonviolence. That mind becomes truly healthy and serves as a source of immense inspiration for yourself and others.

When you acquire a mind such as that, a mind permeated by the blessed meekness referred to by Lord Jesus, you "inherit the earth." You become the master of all the circumstances, conditions, and developments within the material world around you. None of these can pressure your mind any longer. Like a lotus, you bloom above all the conditions of the lake of the world, and remain untouched by them. Like a swan, you sport in the lake of the world, but at any moment you can shake your wings, throw off all the water particles, and fly away.

Thus, when true meekness arises, you attain dominion over the material world. The world of matter does not matter anymore. In Vedantic terminology, you triumph over *maya*, or cosmic illusion, and are no longer tempted by worldly values.

The abundance of the earth is for the desireless, not for the man with desires. When a person approaches the objects of the world with desire, he becomes a slave to them. The objects begin to overpower the person and it becomes impossible for him to possess them in the true sense. Desires create slavery to the objects of the world and a slavish mentality degrades the soul.

But in the state of true meekness, the soul submits itself to God alone. It is not tied to the objects through the strings of desires. Therefore, it recovers its mastery over the earth. It rules matter; it commands circumstances; and it acquires a supreme victory that echoes with an immeasurable sense of inner triumph.

The Song of Saint Chaitanya | Speaking of a the qualities of a saint, the great Indian Saint, Chaitanya, sang: "*Trinaadapi suneechena, tarorapi sahish-nunaa, amaanina maanadena, kirtaniyaa sadaaharih.*"—"He who is humbler than a blade of grass, and yet, more enduring than a tree; he who gives respect to those who lack it—he is ever immersed in singing the praises of the Lord at all times."

These words describe the characteristics of great men, men whose spiritual majesty endows them with utter humility and powerful endurance. Just as blades of grass bend willingly and without complaint beneath the feet of those who walk upon them, a man of true meekness submits himself joyfully to the unfoldment of the Divine Will. Just as a mango tree gives its sweet fruit to a child who throws stones at its branches, or a sandalwood tree gives its exquisite fragrance to the very ax with which it was struck, a man of true meekness radiates a spontaneous tolerance and endurance under all circumstances.

A man of true humility ever delights in making other people feel happy and contented. Because of the spiritual strength that flows to him from within his own heart, he does not seek to draw from others any consolation or sustenance or praise for himself. Rather, he spontaneously showers others with honor, support and encouragement.

One who has reached great spiritual heights experiences such an overpowering sense of internal expansion that ego spontaneously loses all its importance. His mind then flows spontaneously to God at all times.

How Graciously The Tree Bows Down

There is another saying in Sanskrit: *"Namanti phalino vrikshah"*—"A tree that is laden with fruit bows down." The implication of this saying is that when prosperity comes to you, when you are endowed with the blessings of life, humility should develop. If prosperity makes one conceited, that prosperity is unhealthy prosperity, envenomed prosperity—like tasty food which has deadly poison in it.

One who is truly humble and prosperous becomes a flawless instrument in Divine Hands, without ever thinking to take the credit for the miraculous results achieved by the Cosmic Will working through him. "How great is this work that I have done!" is never asserted by one who has attained the blessed state of meekness or humility. In the overflowing sense of fulfillment that accompanies his mental expansion, he knows that it is not the ego, but the Divine Will that works through human beings, producing great wonders.

The Pride of Gods Humbled

The following dramatic story, adapted from *Kenopanishad*, shows how gods learned a powerful lesson in humility. The play takes place in Heaven, where gods move in aerial cars and enjoy celestial glories. There no one grows old, and no one is subject to death. There flowers do not fade, and youth does not depart. There music floods the atmosphere, rivers of honey flow abundantly, and the Kalpaka (wish-yielding) Tree bears the objects of all desires. There in the Heavenly world, great gods such as Indra, Agni, Vayu, Varuna and others attained victory over terrible demons, and each is puffed up with pride and bragging about his greatness.

As our scene opens, Indra is seated on the throne of god, carrying a mace and thunderbolt. The other gods are gathered around him. Fire-god (Agni) has a halo of fire, Wind-god (Vayu) has a halo of clouds and wind, Water-god (Varuna) carries a halo of water. There are other gods as well.

Indra: Verily we have attained victory by our own might. Recall the power of these demons. They were stronger and more valiant than death, they were unconquerable in the three worlds. We have destroyed them. Look at my arms. How heroically did I fight against these demons! My invincible thunderbolt can destroy the three worlds.

Fire God: O Indra, you are the King of kings. You are valiant. I too have immense powers. I have burned down great demons. I have broken their magical influence by my luminosity. I can burn down the three worlds by my effulgence. Who can battle against me? I am most powerful.

Wind-god: Do not brag of your strength before me. It was because of my strength that you gods attained victory over the demons. I can toss the mountains and dislodge the oceans from their seats. I have destoryed these demons by my excellent energy.

Water-god: Verily I am most powerful of all. I can sweep away all the lands in a twinkling of an eye. I have played the most important part in killing these monsters.

Indra: (Standing up with an air of great importance.) Speak not of your strength. I have been the source of your strength and power. Who else in the world is like me? I am the god of all gods. I am lord over the celestials. Look at my arms, look at my thunderbolt.

(A rumbling sound is heard, and there appears before the gods a mighty Yaksha—a strange spirit. The gods are alarmed.)

Indra: O, look, look, who is there!

Fire-god: Surely he is a demon. Let us destroy him.

Wind-god: No, be careful, he shines with infinite strength. He has thousands of hands, thousands of feet. He is truly strange; we have never seen him before.

Water-god: Who knows if he is friend or foe! Let us secure his friendship. Surely we will be undone if we have to fight with him.

Indra: Be calm, O gods. O Jataveda, Fire-god, you are the mightiest of beings. Go to this Yaksha and find out who he is, why he has come here, and whether he is friend or foe. Find out all this and report back to us soon.

Fire-god: I shall do that, my Lord!

(Fire-god approaches the Yaksha.)

Yaksha: (Smiling): Who are you? You walk as if you are the greatest hero.

Fire-god: Don't you know that I am Fire-god?

Yaksha: What is your strength, you who speak with such pride?

Fire-god: I can burn the three worlds in an instant like a straw.

Yaksha: Like a straw? Then burn before me this straw with all your might, or go back where you came from! Let me see the validity of your bragging. (Yaksha puts a straw before Fire-god, who blows with all his might, but cannot burn the straw.)

Fire-god: (to himself) What has happened to my strength? Am I not the Fire-god? Who is this

Yaksha who has humbled me in this manner? (He runs back to Indra.)

Indra: We welcome you back, Agni. Tell us all about the Yaksha.

Fire-god: (Dejected) I do not know what the Yaksha is?

Indra: So, all your bragging was like the tinkling of brass. You vain braggart! You, Wind-god, you are proud of your strength, go and find out who that Yaksha is.

(Wind-god approaches Yaksha with great pride)

Yaksha: (Smiling) Who are you? You walk as if you can toss the whole world.

Wind-god: Don't you know that I am Matarishwan, the supporter of the whole world? Without me no one can live. If I wish I can blow out the whole universe even like a small ball, or like a straw.

Yaksha: Very well. Do not brag before me. I am not a believer in empty words. Show me your strength by blowing away this simple piece of straw.

(The Wind-god blows with all his might, but he cannot blow away the straw.)

Wind-god: (To himself) I have become powerless before this Spirit! I have no strength? (In despair he runs back to Indra.)

Indra: Welcome, O Wind-god. Tell me, who is that Yaksha?

Wind-god: (With dejected face) O Lord, I could not show any strength before this Being. I do not know who that Spirit is.

Indra: (Laughing) So, Wind-god, your power is of no purpose. You too are a vain braggart. (Turning to Water-god) And now, O Varuna, you who are the mighty god of waters, go to this Yaksha and find out who he is.

Water-god: Very well, my Lord. I shall follow your command and exhibit my might.

(He approaches Yaksha with proud steps.)

Yaksha: (Smiling) Who are you, who walks like a mad elephant intoxicated with pride?

Water-god: (With a rumbling voice) I am the Water-god. I can drown the whole world in waters. I am the mightiest of gods. I am amazed that you do not know me!

Yaksha: I am not a believer in vain and empty words. Show me your strength. Try to drown this simple straw if you can.

(Water-god tries again and again, exhibiting all his strength, but to no avail.)

Water-god: (to himself) Woe is me! My strength has gone. Let me run away as the others have done. (He runs back to Indra.) O Indra, I do not know what that Yaksha is. I am deprived of all my strength.

Indra: (Laughing) So, all of you have proved powerless over that Yaksha! Never brag again of your strength, little gods. I will myself go to find out who that Yaksha is.

(Indra advances towards the Yaksha and, as he does so, the Yaksha disappears. But in its place there appears Uma, the shining Goddess, decked with a golden crown, carrying a scripture in one hand and a flower in another.)

Indra: (Bewildered, his eyes dazzled by the effulgent glory of Uma) O Goddess, did you see where that Yaksha has gone? He was here a few minutes ago. Who is He?

Uma: O Indra, the Yaksha is none other than *Brahman* Himself. It was by His help that you conquered the demons. You have developed vanity. You have no strength of your own. It is the strength of *Brahman* that helped you to attain victory over the demons. You have forgotten *Brahman*, the Self. Surrender to that Supreme Being and give up pride. Know the Lord and be humble.

Indra: O, how sinful am I! I forgot the Lord who assisted me in all my victories. Without Him even the greatest of gods cannot move even a straw. O Mother, O Goddess of Wisdom, be gracious towards me and bestow upon me everlasting devotion to the Lord. Illumine my mind with the light of true knowledge. I have surrendered unto Thee.

This dramatic story from *Kenopanishad* illustrates how pride is a terrible enemy of spiritual knowledge. When the gods began to glorify themselves because of their victory over the demons, the Divine Self presented Himself in the form of a mysterious Yaksha to rid them of pride and confer on them true insight into the essential nature of *Atman*.

Fire-god, Wind-god, and Water-god are symbolic of intellect (mind included), *pranas* (senses included), and *chitta* (unconscious) respectively. Ego is represented by Indra—the Lord of gods. The parable shows that the intellect, mind, *pranas* and senses are unable to attain the knowledge of the Self.

However, when Indra moves towards *Brahman*, the vison of Yaksha disappears. When ego rids itself of false pride, and pursues the enquiry of "Who am I?," the exaggerated perception of the Self that seemed to baffle the mind, senses, intellect, and *pranas* vanishes from view. There arises the dawning of spiritual wisdom in the form of Goddess Uma.

With the appearance of the Goddess—the intuitive unfoldment of the intellect—an aspirant is able to discover the true nature of the Self, by Whose power and sustenance all the internal and external instruments of the soul perform their diverse functions. Like a river merging in the ocean the sense of individuality merges in *Brahman*. This is liberation—the goal of one's existence.

The Pride of the Pandavas Humbled

In the *Mahabharata*, the five Pandava brothers represent the forces of virtue, while their cousins, the Kauravas, represent the forces of evil. The following three stories from this great scripture highlight the manner in which three of the Pandava brothers received profound lessons in humility which helped them grow in wisdom and spiritual strength:

Bhima's Lesson in Humility

At one time during the twelve year period in which the Pandavas were living in the forest, Arjuna went away to the heavenly world to attain the celestial weapons necessary to guarantee victory in the future confrontation with the Kauravas. While Arjuna was away, his brothers and Draupadi visited great pilgrimage centers in the Himalayas. One day, at the great holy shrine of Badrikedar, a northeastern puff of wind brought a flower of exquisite beauty and it fell right near Draupadi. Captivated by the beauty and the fragrance of that flower, Draupadi asked Bhima to bring her more of them. Eager to fulfill Draupadi's request, Bhima set out in the direction from which the flower had been carried by the wind.

Endowed with superhuman strength and capacities of which he was exceedingly proud, Bhima was able to cross mountains and forests at breakneck speed and he quickly arrived in a plantain grove near the region presided over by Kubera, the god of treasure. There, in that grove, Bhima encountered a gigantic old monkey lying across his path and blocking his passage.

When Bhima asked that monkey to move aside, the monkey said that he was too old to move and that if Bhima was so interested in passing that way he should just move his tail and pass on. Annoyed with the old monkey, Bhima arrogantly started to lift its tail, but he could not stir it. Summoning all his strength, he became full of perspiration and began to choke, and yet that tail did not budge an inch.

Bhima thought to himself that this could not be an ordinary creature, and suddenly filled with humility, he bowed down before that monkey, inquiring about his real nature.

The monkey then introduced himself as Hanuman, the leader of the monkey army in Rama's time, and proceeded to tell Bhima all about the events in Treta Yuga that led to the eventual defeat of Ravana. In the course of their conversation, Hanuman revealed to Bhima the majestic cosmic form he had assumed when he crossed the ocean. The intention of Hanuman that day in the forest was to meet Bhima, to test his strength and bestow upon him his blessings. The two—Bhima and Hanuman—were actually brothers. Hanuman was the son of the wind-god during Treta Yuga, when Rama was born, and Bhima was the son of the wind-god in Dwapara Yuga, when Krishna was born.

Bhima was immensely delighted to have met Hanuman, and when Hanuman affectionately took Bhima in his arms, Bhima felt that a new energy emerged in his body and he became much stronger than ever before. Although Bhima had been renowned for his great strength and was quite proud of that strength, he learned from his encounter with Hanuman the majestic power of cosmic energy, of cosmic *prana*. Before that energy that sustains and empowers every individual, the power of his egoistic personality was but little.

Yudhishthira's Lesson in Humility

During the Mahabharata War, Dronacharya began to employ celestial weapons against the army of the Pandavas, although using such devastating weapons against ordinary soldiers was considered highly unrighteous in those days. Seeing the terrible devastation brought about by these sinful methods, Lord Krishna resolved to bring the power of Dronacharya to an end by employing a form of Divine deception.

Dronacharya was endowed with such tremendous power that he was considered virtually unconquerable. However, he had great attachment to his son, Ashwatthama, and that attachment made him vulnerable. Lord Krishna explained to the Pandavas that only if Dronacharya were to learn of the death of this dear son would he be overwhelmed with sufficient grief to lay down his arms and stop fighting.

With Krishna's words in mind, Bhima killed an elephant named Ashwatthama and then cried out, "Ashwatthama is dead." When Dronacharya heard this, he became deeply upset, but could not believe that it was his son who had been killed. He asserted that he would not believe this terrible news unless he heard it uttered directly by Yudhishthira, who was well-known for his unflinching devotion to truth.

At this point, Krishna persuaded Yudhishthira to come forward and confirm the death of Ashwatthama. With great reluctance, Yudhishthira brought his chariot within the hearing range of Dronacharya and shouted, "Ashwatthama has been killed." When Yudhishthira was about to softly add, "Not man, but elephant," the sounds of the battle-field drowned out those qualifying words before Dronacharya could hear them.

Thus convinced that it was his son who had indeed been killed, Dronacharya sadly laid down his arms and vowed to fast unto death. Seeing the guru they had once loved in this pathetic situation, the Pandavas would merely have taken him prisoner; but to the horror of all, Dhrishtadyumna rushed forward and quickly beheaded Dronacharya while he sat in meditation.

In this story about the deceiving of Dronacharya, the *Mahabharata* brings out a subtle point regarding virtue—that the principles of ethics are not as black and white as they would seem. The words that Krishna persuaded Yudhishthira to speak to Dronacharya were apparently untrue, but at the same time they were necessary to bring about the ultimate victory of the forces of virtue.

Practising a virtue such as truthfulness is not a matter of laying down some laws and following them literally, mathematically. The practice of virtue requires a complex handling of the mind and deep philosophical insight. Although one may speak what seems true, if that "truth" does not serve the greater long-range purpose of the Divine plan, then it is actually falsehood. If that "truth" is in conflict with a higher truth, then it should not be uttered, or it should be watered down or refashioned with wisdom. For Yudhishthira to gain this understanding, his subtle spiritual pride about being the paragon of truthfulness had to be quelled.

Throughout his life, Yudhishthira had faithfully adhered to the concept of speaking the truth as he saw it, and he was well-known for his vow never to utter a lie. In Yudhishthira, as well as in any spiritual aspirant, such a vow to pursue the ethical injunction of *satyam*, or truthfulness, is indeed praiseworthy. However, in the earlier stages of spiritual evolution such a vow is generally tinged with egoistic pride and made with a shallow intellectual understanding that must give way to more profound wisdom as one advances. So it was with Yudhishthira.

To make Yudhishthira aware of these erroneous concepts hidden in his unconscious and help him eliminate them, Krishna brought out the weakness in front of thousands of great heroes. Thereby, he helped Yudhishthira purify himself more effectively and move on to higher levels of understanding. Thus, through the intervention of Krishna, the personality of Yudhishthira became more integrated; at the same time, Dronacharya was destroyed and the eventual victory of the Pandavas was made more secure.

Arjuna's Lesson in Humility — Before Krishna passed away, he requested that Arjuna take care of the women and children that were left behind after he and the Yadava heroes were all gone. Rushing to honor that request, Arjuna hurried to Dwaraka to gather his charges before the city of Dwaraka sank into the ocean.

While Arjuna was escorting the women and children towards Hastinapur, a large gang of robbers attacked them. At that time, Arjuna tried to use all the weapons that had previously been at his command, but found that his power had been rendered ineffective. Experiencing tremendous frustration and humiliation, Arjuna could only watch as their wealth was looted and most of the women were carried off by the marauders. In despair, he brought the remainder of the survivors to safety and gave them shelter in various regions of the kingdom.

Overwhelmed with sorrow after seeing his inability to save all the women and children of Dwaraka, and not knowing where to turn for consolation, Arjuna went to the *ashram* of Sage Vyasa. Approaching the sage, he said, "How was it possible for five hundred thousand great Yadava heroes to be destroyed in such a short time? How was it possible that I could not protect the Yadava women from ordinary robbers despite all my efforts?"

Under the guidance of Sage Vyasa, Arjuna was then led to understand that in all the events surrounding the destruction of the Yadavas, as well as in all the events that occurred during the great war, it was the Divine plan that was unfolding according to the will of Krishna.

Vyasa explained that when Krishna's mission as an *avatara* (Divine Incarnation) was over, he and all his people had to depart. If Krishna had wanted to save his relatives, he could have done so; but, since their work in this world was over, he allowed them all to be destroyed. The women that were captured by those robbers also were following their *karmas*. They had been *apsaras* in the heavenly world who, because of certain errors, had been cursed to enter into human embodiment and remain there until robbers released them from that bondage.

Thus, Vyasa helped Arjuna realize that it was Divine will, not the egoistic will of an individual, that was of uppermost importance in this drama of the world-process. It was not his own strength that really won the battles for him, nor his own weakness that lost them. It was the Divine Krishna, driving the chariot who rendered their enemies lifeless; he, Arjuna, was merely acting as an instrument of Krishna's will.

Becoming Free of Ego

For the vast majority of people, ego IS one's identity. Relaxation of ego is achieved only during sleep, when ego is set aside not by one's choice, but by an unconscious, biological process.

But when you are moving from normal to supernormal awareness, you begin to discover that ego is not the source of your inspiration and your initiative. In reality you are different from your ego. As that understanding grows, you learn to set aside the ego by your own choice through increasing intuitional understanding.

The art of becoming free of ego is indeed the subtlest art. However, it is acquired through a persistant process of personality integration by which you bring renewed health to your body, and to your conscious and unconscious mind. If you are physically healthy it is possible for you to detach from the body. If you are mentally healthy and serene, then it is possible for you to detach yourself from the mind. If your unconscious is not pressured by impure subtle desires, then it is possible for you to go beyond your ego.

As you balance yourself by right action, devotion, meditation, reflection, and of course, *satsanga* or good association, you begin to develop a harmonized personality. You realize that relaxing the ego is not so difficult, and begin to feel as if your spirit is a bird flying through the newly opened window of a cage, free to soar beyond all limitations.

In daily life, therefore, one should be alert not to let pride, conceit and egoism become prominent. You must subjugate the promptings of the ego day by day, and feel humbler than a blade of grass and yet mightier than mountains; lesser than a little glow worm, and yet more effulgent than the sun.

The flowers do not advertise their fragrance. The sun has no need to proclaim its luminosity by beating drums. The ocean has no need to sing the praises of its own profundity. The Himalayas have no need to brag about their lofty heights. So too, an aspirant who unfolds the fragrance of virtue, unravels the luminosity of spiritual wisdom, experiences the profundity of universal life, and ascends the heights of superconsciousness has no need to indulge in pride and its numerous expressions.

DELUSION
(MOHA)

The term *moha* is usually defined as delusion, or an obscuring of reasoning, but delusion has many implications. In the highest philosophical sense, it is *moha* that causes the unenlightened mind to perceive a world of multiplicity, when in reality nothing exists other than the nondual *Brahman*—the Absolute Self. It is *moha* that causes the mind to ignore the blazing Reality of Divine glory that permeates all and to become stuck to names and forms; to ignore the ocean but become attached to the waves; to ignore the sky and become attached to little clouds.

Moha causes the mind to be caught up by apparent values of family and society, and then to feel completely confined to those values and circumstances. It is *moha* that causes you to view yourself as an individual completely dependent on your family or friends, and to feel that your joy completely depends upon them and theirs upon you.

Ishwara Shrishti Versus Jiva Shrishti

Imagine for a moment that you live in a beautifully decorated palatial home and, feeling a bit lazy, you lay down on your luxurious velvety bed. You doze off, only to discover that in your dream you are being chased by a tiger. No one is there to help you, and no matter where you run you are miserable. On waking, you realize that it was all just a dream. There was no tiger and your life was not in danger at all.

That palatial room with its velvety bed is symbolic of what the scriptures refer to as *Ishwara shrishti*—the creation of God. The Divine creation is majestic and infinitely blissful. From morning to night, the immense glory of God cascades through this universe, permeating all, internally and externally.

The dream that arose when you went to sleep, the dream in which you found yourself entangled in so many difficulties, is symbolic of *jiva shrishti*—the creation of the individual. Despite the omnipresent abundance of the Divine creation, the human mind remains cramped by the alternating pleasure and pain of life. Due to its conditioning and limitation, the mind experiences a world of time and space and is unable to bask in the awareness of Divine Presence. This is due to *moha*.

Moha, Maya and the Three Gunas

In the *Gita*, Chapter Seven, Verse 13, Lord Krishna speaks about the deluding power of the three *gunas* (modes of nature): *"Tribhirgunamayair bhaavairebhis sarvamidam jagat; Mohitam naabhijaanaati maamebhyah paramavyayam"*—"Deluded by these three modes of nature, all this world does not know Me who am different from them and immutable."

This world is created by the blend of three *gunas: sattwa, rajas* and *tamas.* On the psychological plane, when you become calm, relaxed, and aware of Divine Presence, there is *sattwa* in your mind. When mind becomes free of anger, hate, and greed and filled with Divine qualities, a window to eternity opens within your heart. You discover a mysterious source of inner peace. *Sattwa* beckons you to that.

When you are agitated and distracted, unable to be one-pointed, filled with ambitions, hypocritical and ostentatious, *rajas* is predominating in your personality. When you become prone to irrationality, bitterness, frustration, pervasive pessimism, anger, and hate and your mind loses all spiritual sensitivity, *tamas* has taken over your mind.

A Family Of Thieves   Sri Ramakrishna Paramahamsa told a parable about a king who was traveling alone, carrying a great treasure with him. Seeing him vulnerable to attack, three thieves sneaked up behind him, robbed him, tied him up, and dumped him in a dry well.

In a while, however, one of the three thieves developed compassion for the king. While the other two thieves were away, he secretly came back and untied him. Then he guided the king to the edge of the forest, and said, "Now you are free to go." The king responded, "Why don't you come with me? You helped me to be free of that bondage. Come to visit me and I will reward you with lots of treasure." The thief said, "No, your majesty, I belong to the family of thieves, and I have no access in your royal palace."

The implication of the parable is that all three of the *gunas*—*sattwa, rajas,* and *tamas*—are thieves. They attack the soul, which is essentially the emperor of emperors—the Divine Self—and rob it of its glory and majesty. Then they tie it up with the fetters of illusion and throw it into the dry well of repeated embodiment. The thief that develops compassion towards the soul is *sattwa.* He can lead it to liberation, but that is as far as he can go. As a member of the family of thieves, he belongs to the relative world and cannot transcend it.

It is easy to see how *rajas* and *tamas* are like thieves that keep you tied up with illusion. But how can it be that *sattwa*, the highest *guna*, also deludes?

When *sattwa* visits the mind for only a short duration, when it comes as a "guest" once in a while, it causes delusion. When you are not accustomed to the presence of *sattwa*, you erroneously conclude that the happiness it brings to you comes from the objects or situations that are outside of you at the moment. It makes you want to secure those objects and leads you into a state of dependency and bondage. On the other hand, if *sattwa* is allowed to stay with you, to abide in your personality, then that *sattwa* promotes enlightenment. Such abiding *sattwa* opens the door to internal reflection and shows you that happiness is coming from within yourself. So you plan to find a guru, to get into *satsanga* (good association) and to promote that *sattwa* more and more.

Insight
Into Maya

When *rajas* and *tamas* dominate your mind, the deluding force of *maya* or cosmic illusion increases and *moha* swells up. Everything is colored by illusion. But when *sattwa* increases, the deluding force of *maya* diminishes, and fetters break.

Maya has two aspects: *avidya* (ignorance) and *vidya* (knowledge). *Avidya* drives you into more and more ignorance, increased involvement in the world of time and space. It keeps you bound to thinking of the past or planning for the future. Under its sway, you do not have even a moment's rest nor the peace of mind to transcend your ego and discover the joys of eternity.

While *avidya* holds you down in the world of relativity, *vidya* lifts you up. Using the simile of the Christian cross, *avidya* keeps you horizontal, always pressured by the past, moving towards the future. *Vidya* gives you a vertical lift. Spiritual knowledge enables you to rise above the limited world of time and space and transcend it.

Everyone in this world who has not attained enlightenment is as if fettered by chains, and in a fettered condition moves from one embodiment to another. In Sanskrit, fetters are known as *pashas*, and therefore, the scriptures refer to human beings in this predicament as *pashus* (animals) and to God as *Pashu Pati*, the Lord of all the animals. Therefore, in order to escape the delusive aspect of *maya*, in order to get out of the world of time and space, *sattwa* has to be promoted and *rajas* and *tamas* have to be controlled and sublimated.

Don't Let Yourself Be Tied Up by Moha

Moha and *mamata* (the sense of mine-ness) put shackles on the feet of your soul. Bound by *moha* and *mamata*, the soul that could have experienced infinity and eternity becomes confined instead to the small circumference of its attachments in the realm of time and space. This point is simply illustrated in the following parable:

Once a king had a pet hawk that used to fly freely and enjoy its freedom. In the course of its daily flight, the hawk began to perch upon the hut of an old woman. The lady in that little hut used to have some fragrant hot pudding cooking and she would open the window and talk to the hawk.

"O dear little one," she would coax, "Come to me and I will feed you and keep you warm, for you must be feeling very cold out there."

At first, the hawk was merely amused by her soft words and would fly off after a brief rest. As days passed, however, he began to think, "How cozy it must be inside the hut. It really is cold out here, and maybe I do deserve a little extra warmth. Surely it would be so nice to have someone take care of me." So, with these thoughts in his mind, the hawk flew through the window into the old lady's hut.

Immediately the old lady caught the hawk and tied its legs well so that he could not slip out into the wilderness again. Then she began to feed the hawk some of her delicacies. For an hour or so the hawk felt very comfortable. Soon, however, he began to think of the freedom that he used to have. All the while the old lady went on saying to the hawk, "Now look how wonderful life is: no more running wildly, no more flying everywhere. You are mommy's boy now."

Meanwhile, the king began to miss his hawk and he embarked on a search mission. As he passed the little hut in the forest he looked through the window and, lo and behold, to his great surprise saw his pet hawk with his legs tied! "O little hawk," he cried out, "What misery have you brought upon yourself by your delusion!"

Like the hawk in this parable, the human spirit, which is always essentially beyond all confines, repeatedly accepts a condition of limitation. It is your birthright to fly freely everywhere, yet you somehow become accustomed to living in a cage, like a bird that has forgotten the joys of freedom.

Crossing the River of Moha

A popular story about Tulasidas, the saintly author of the *Ramayana*, gives humorous yet poignant insight into the tricks played by the mind due to infatuation or exaggerated attachment. This aspect of *moha* hinders an individual's practical sense, while it also leads him away from that which is conducive to spiritual advancement:

When Tulasidas was a young man, he became strongly attracted to a young lady and married her. Soon he became so enamored of his wife that he forgot everything else. According to the story, shortly after they were married Tulasidas' wife had to go to her parents' home for awhile. During that time young Tulasidas, feeling that he could not live without her, decided to visit the house where his wife was staying in a village just across the river.

During a stormy night in the rainy season, Tulasidas set out on his mission. When he reached the river, he found something there in the darkness that he thought was a raft; so he sat down upon it and rowed. Actually it was not a raft at all, but a dead body! However, due to his haste, Tulasidas never realized this.

After he crossed the river, Tulasidas went to the house where his wife lived. To his dismay, everything was locked up for the night. Thus, the next challenge before him was reaching the upper story of the little building where he would find her sleeping.

Tulasidas saw what he thought was a rope hanging on the building and he caught hold of the rope and climbed up. It was not a rope, however, but a snake—but Tulasidas did not realize that till the early morning! Finally, when he knocked at his wife's door, she was amazed to see him. Rebuking him, she said, "You could have waited; why did you come like this? If you had as much love for the Lord as you have for me, a mortal person, you would have attained God-realization by now!"

This unexpected rebuke from his wife made the mind of Tulasidas immediately reflective and awakened many of his previous spiritual *samskaras* (impressions). He realized how, pressured by his desires, he had not known what he was doing during the night: he had considered a dead body as a raft, and a coiled snake as a rope! He was awed by the power of his mind to do seemingly impossible things under the sway of desires. So if the same type of longing were to be directed towards God, one could attain liberation in a very short time.

Thus reflecting after being rebuked by his wife, Tulasidas suddenly experienced an internal awakening and made a resolve, a *samkalpa*, to attain God-realization. He realized how foolish it was for him to have devoted all his energy to things that are transient, and vowed to direct his sentiments only towards Lord Rama.

Step Out of the Waters of Delusion

The great message of all spiritual teaching is that you have a choice: you can either keep ducking into the stream of ignorance and move from illusion to illusion, or you can enter the stream of knowledge and recapture your essential identity as the Divine Self. Reflect upon this story about Narada and his experience in the turbulent waters of *moha*:

Once upon a time, Sage Narada went to Vaikuntha, where Lord Vishnu dwells. When the Sage entered, Vishnu welcomed him warmly, but, to Narada's surprise, Goddess Lakshmi put a veil before her face and turned away from him. Dismayed and perplexed, Narada asked Lord Vishnu, "Why did Goddess turned away from me—I who am so pure minded, a person of great austerity?"

Lord Vishnu replied, "The ways of the Goddess are mysterious. She is the embodiment of *maya*, or cosmic illusion, and thus very difficult to understand, O Narada. So too, one never knows the subtle delusion that operates through one's unconscious."

Narada then pleaded before Lord Vishnu, "Oh Lord, show me your *maya*. Let me understand what it is." Lord Vishnu said, "Very well. Soon I shall explain it to you, but let us go for a ride and relax for awhile in the heavenly world first."

He then invoked the presence of the great bird Garuda, who swiftly appeared and carried them through the blue sky until they came to a beautiful and enchanting place, abounding with crystal-clear streams and trees laden with blossoms.

There Lord Vishnu said, "Let us take a plunge in this wonderful stream and then rest," said Lord Vishnu. "You go first, Narada." "Yes my Lord," said Narada, and he handed Lord Vishnu his *vina*, a stringed instrument he carried with him wherever he went.

Then Narada entered the water. The moment he put his head under the water, his whole personality and body changed, transformed by *maya*. When he emerged, there was no Lord Vishnu, no Narada— there was only a beautiful lady, well-dressed and bewildered by her presence in the water, not knowing where she came from or who she was.

As she stood there in confusion, King Taladhwaja passed by with his royal retinue as they were engaged in a hunting expedition through the forest. Suddenly he saw the lady and was immediately enchanted by her beauty. "Who are you?" said Taladhwaja. The lady replied, "Oh King, I do not know." The King proposed that she become his Queen, and the lady agreed because she felt so alone and did not have any protector.

Thus the lady became the supermost Queen of the great King, who loved her the most of all his wives. Time passed, and the lady, whose name became Saubhagya Sundari, remained completely unaware that she was essentially Narada. In the course of time she bore twelve sons, one after the other. As these sons were growing up, the lady, who was really Narada, was constantly involved in solving the problems in her large family—tending to quarrels, celebrating birthdays, caring for sickness, delighting in their attainments.

In the course of time, a powerful enemy attacked the kingdom. In order to meet that enemy and his vast army, the King, along with his sons, went out to battle. And a fierce battle it was, resulting in the death of all the royal sons of Saubhagya Sundari. The King, however, although badly defeated, escaped death.

When the Queen came to know of the defeat of her husband and the destruction of her family, she experienced intense grief. She rushed to the battlefield to see the bodies of her sons, whom she loved so dearly, and there she grieved even more intensely.

At that time, Lord Vishnu, in the form of an old ascetic, appeared before her saying, "Oh lady, why do you grieve? This is the nature of things. All that is born must die. Further, by grieving, you do not help the departed souls. You should rather enter the water of this stream and perform rituals and prayers for the peace of those souls."

The queen plunged into the stream and as she emerged she found herself again transformed into Narada. Lord Vishnu was there smiling, holding the *vina* of the Sage in his hand. He said, "Oh Sage, why did you spend such a long time in the water?" And Narada realized then, with great wonder, that all his experiences had been nothing but the mysterious workings of *maya*.

Essentially, we are all Saint Narada; we are all Divine, free of all sorrow and misery. But when we enter the stream of *avidya* or ignorance, the enchanting stream of the conditioned mind, we are transformed into a *jiva*, or individualized soul.

As an individualized soul, you become wedded to your ego, involved in the world of *moha* and *mamata* (mine-ness), and spend your years struggling to find solutions for problems in the world of time and space—where there are no permanent solutions for anything.

Absorbed in *"moha's* empire"—your family, friends and material possessions—you find it natural to think that these are the only things of importance. As a result, you live only for these perishable things, not realizing that you are essentially the Spirit, beyond time and space.

Through spiritual *sadhana* (discipline), however, you eventually develop *vairagya* (dispassion)
and realize that everything will pass away. Nothing
that you depend upon can be dependable all the
time. You gain insight into the subtle and mysterious
workings of *maya*, and strive to learn the art of mystic
awakening.

When your personality has been fully integrated,
you are led to another kind of stream: *jnana ganga*,
or the stream of wisdom and knowledge. The moment you enter into that stream, you emerge in your
own essential form. As if awakened from the sway of
Lord Vishnu's *maya*, you find the Divine Self smiling
before you. You cast off the illusion of the sense of
individuality, and emerge as *Brahman*. All your miseries and sorrows, all the experiences of countless
embodiments, fade from your view like the experiences of a long dream. Then you realize, "I am
Brahman—the Absolute Self."

The Story of Punya and Pavana

In each embodiment you view yourself as born
into a particular family with a particular history of
prosperity and adversity. As you grow you build your
own empire of family and friends. But when you die
and move on to another embodiment, all those
realities are forgotten and new ones take their place.

In *Yoga Vasistha* there is a story of two brothers,
Punya and Pavana, who were sons of very saintly
parents. When their parents died, grief invaded

their minds. However, Punya was older and had studied the *Vedic* scriptures. He began to reflect upon the teachings that he had received from his father and he attained enlightenment.

Pavana could not give up his grief, so his elder brother, showering his compassion, said, "O my brother, why are you grieving? You are greiving for our departed parents, but what about the parents of your previous embodiments? You should be grieving for a thousand fathers and a thousand mothers! We

have not lost just one father and one mother. In every embodiment there were parents who were just as dear. Why aren't you grieving for all of them?"

In other words, in each of your thousands of embodiment you had so many people you loved and depended upon, so many who depended on you. Then, when you moved out of each embodiment, you left those realities completely behind. Now. in your present embodiment, you might have been reborn in the very same town in which you had previously died, and every day you walk by your old house and see your grownup sons and daughters. But now you simply pass by disinterestedly, and you have nothing to do with their problems. New attachments have taken their place.

Breaking the spell of delusion is the purpose of existence. Unless you break it you cannot enjoy the blessings of God that pour down at every moment in this world. Divine Grace pours down like monsoon rains, but if the cup of your heart is inverted due to *moha*, not a single drop goes into it. Straighten it up, and surely you will find that "your cup runneth over." That sound of your spirit overflowing with Divine grace is the most beautiful sound imaginable!

Hear the Splashing Waters of Eternity

Once a man crossed the desert in hot summer, parched with thirst. He came upon a high stone wall and climbed to the top. Looking down, he saw the surging water of a beautiful river.

The sight of water was so delightful to his mind; but how, he thought, could he get to that water from the heights of the wall? Suddenly he realized that the wall was not so strong, and he could loosen its stones and throw them down. He started doing that, and each time a stone fell the water splashed. With each sound of splashing water, great joy entered his mind.

The river below called out to him, "Why do you pelt stones at me?" He said, "Do not be angry with me. As I break these stones the wall is coming down and I am coming closer to you. The splashing sound is very pleasing to my ears because I know that soon I will drink your water."

Like the man in this parable, everyone has been travelling through the desert of the world-process and has climbed a high wall of illusion. Whatever happiness you have experienced is a kind of mirage. When you become aware of your real predicament you realize how thirsty you are, and you begin to understand the value of breaking the illusion.

When you have philosophical insight, the breaking of illusions is not the painful process that the masses consider it to be. Rather, it is like the tumbling down of the wall in our parable. The falling stones allow you to listen to the splashing water of eternity. They remind you that the world of time and space is not your real and permanent home. Therefore, you must live your life in such a way that the world around you does not cripple your mind. Allow your mind to expand as the breaking illusions bring you closer and closer to the water of eternity.

Overcoming Moha

In Chapter Seven of the *Gita*, verse 14, Lord Krishna says: "This Divine Maya of Mine, composed of the three *gunas*, is difficult to cross over, but those who surrender to Me, they alone are able to cross it."

This world of *maya*, of *moha*, is like an ocean in which everyone is bobbing up and down, driven from one whirlpool to another. One who surrenders to God has found a ship and is being taken on the right course towards life's destination—Self-realization. When the surrender reaches a higher level you have found a jet plane, and when it becomes still higher, a rocket carries you irretrievably beyond the world's gravitational pull.

Because of *moha*, you turn away from the Divine, although the Divine is the very fabric of the universe, the very reality behind all things. As you turn away from God you are whipped by the delusive force of *maya* more and more. On the other hand, when you come closer to God, the force of *maya* diminishes and you begin to enjoy a sense of equanimity at all times. When you are embued with Divine Love, the force of *maya* will not delude you. The very same world of *maya* begins to show you the right path.

Of great importance in overcoming *moha* is *satsanga* or good-association. In the *Ramayana*, Saint Tulsidas says, "Without *satsanga* and without listening to the glory of God, *moha* will not be driven away, *moha* continues. But if you enjoy *satsanga* and listen to the Divine teachings, then *moha* begins to diminish. If *moha* does not move away from you, you do not reach the Divine abode and you do not enjoy profound devotion."

Thus, overcoming *moha* requires a profound process of Yoga that includes devotion to God, repetition of Divine name, good association, meditation, profound reflection, selfless service, and a great change in your attitude towards others. While serving or loving a family member or friend, try to understand that you are worshiping God through that person. The idea, "He is my son, or she is my daughter" should not cripple your mind. Through every soul you serve, you are serving God. Through every wave you are looking at the ocean. As these attitudes develop, you make decisive strides towards breaking the fetters of *moha*.

In your zeal to break these fetters, be careful not to break the *moha* of others with a hammer. Be gentle toward the delusion of others and do not <u>force</u> them to give it up, although you may try to pursuade them in a loving manner to do so.

However, have no respect for your own delusion. Get the biggest hammer possible and go on breaking it down, eagerly listening to the joyous sound of the splashing water as illusion after illusion falls into it, freeing you of all limitation and leading you to eternity.

JEALOUSY
(MATSARYA)

There are three terms in Sanskrit for jealousy: *irshya, asuya* and *matsarya*.

Irshya refers to the common, relatively mild form of jealousy that people feel day by day when they perceive that someone else is surpassing them— unfairly so!—in matters such as looks, popularity, fame, wealth, happiness and sometimes even spiritual advancement.

Interestingly enough, it is *irshya* which helps sustain movement in the average person's life. If there were no jealousy, many people would wake up lazily and decide to stay in bed all day. Jealousy makes them get up fast and work harder. This form of jealousy plays some positive role in life because it spurs one on to make self-effort and move forward. However, *irshya* itself is a *rajasic* sentiment—a product of a distracted and restless mind—and, as such, must be sublimated on the way to real progress and prosperity.

When *irshya* becomes increasingly *tamasic* or impure, it assumes the form of *asuya* and then *matsarya.* When seeing another person happier or more successful than you causes your heart to burn, jealousy has become more *tamasic* and has assumed its more perverted and gross form as *asuya.* This form of jealousy is accompanied by an urge to degrade the other person, to pursue his defects in order to soothe your own mind. Backbiting and scandal-mongering are often associated with *asuya.*

Matsarya is still more destructive and perverse. Not only do you feel a burning sensation in your heart, but you start seriously planning what to do in order to hurt the person towards whom you are jealous. Obsessed with the idea that his very existence has become a source of misery, a threat to your happiness in life, you become intensely involved in destroying, hurting and removing the person from your way.

Jealousy and Its Ramifications

Jealousy is generally associated with many negative traits of personality. It directs a person to be fraudulent and insincere with those around him, and promotes irritability, anger, hatred, cruelty and pride. It degrades the mind by obstructing the feeling of cosmic love. Like a mental fever, it saps out the energy and vitality of man.

If you study the history of human beings from ancient times, you will see how the *tamasic* form of jealousy has caused great devastation. Such jealousy destroys harmony among family members, friends and neighbors, co-workers, nations and even among aspirants in ashrams (spiritual centers). Jealousy is a great enemy of culture and progress among human beings. It has ruined many homes, frustrated many hopes and broken many hearts.

The Jealousy of Queen Kaikeyi

One of the most poignant examples of the devastating and far-reaching effects of jealousy is found in the *Ramayana*:

One day after the marriage of his sons, at a time when all forms of prosperity flowed to Ayodhya like rivers flowing into the ocean with abundant water during the rains, King Dasharatha approached Guru Vasistha and expressed his cherished desire to see Prince Rama declared the successor or heir apparent to the throne. Sage Vasistha agreed readily and plans to enthrone Rama were begun, bringing delight to all the king's ministers and royal officers. When the news reached the inner chambers of the palace where Queens Kaushalya and Sumitra dwelled, they too were overjoyed and joined in the preparations.

Seeing the great rejoicing in Ayodhya, the gods in the heavens became distressed because they feared that once Rama became king he would no longer be interested in killing Ravana (the Lord of demons), which was the purpose for which they had promoted his incarnation in the first place. Thus, they approached Goddess Saraswati (the Deity presiding over intellect and speech) and appealed to Her to find a way to prevent Rama from becoming coronated, while at the same time sending him into forest life so he would perform his heroic deeds of eradicating demons.

Finally overcome by the pleading of the gods, Saraswati Devi thought of a unique scheme to accomplish their objective and came to the earth plane in search of a person whose intellect could be twisted against Rama. However, she found the minds of all people so eager for his coronation that it was only after extensive searching that Goddess Saraswati found one petty-minded personality—the hunched-backed maid-servant of Kaikeyi, whose name was Manthara—who could be manipulated to plant a seed of discontent against Rama.

Thus, one day when Manthara was in her own room, she heard the sounds of celebration in the streets and asked what was going on. Because her mistress, Queen Kaikeyi, lived in a separate palace, the news of the coronation had not yet reached them. Also King Dasharatha had planned to inform his dear Kaikeyi about this delightful surprise in person but had not yet had the opportunity to do so. When Manthara heard from others that Rama was to be crowned, her heart burned with jealousy due to the secret influence of Goddess Saraswati. Why, she kept asking herself, should Rama, the son of Kaushalya, be coronated instead of Bharata, the son of her mistress, Kaikeyi? With her twisted intellect, the maid-servant then began to plot what she could do to upset the plans for the coronation so that Bharata would be favored for the royal honor instead of Rama.

With this in mind, Manthara approached Queen Kaikeyi with a dejected countenance and then started shedding tears. She then informed Kaikeyi that Rama was about to be coronated, but in conveying that news she created a scenario that would arouse jealousy in the heart of the Queen. With great effort, she convinced her mistress that the king had deliberately sent her own son, Bharata, away from Ayodhya to visit Kaikeyi's parents at that time, and that he had deliberately chosen not to tell Kaikeyi about the coronation as part of a plan to degrade and humiliate Kaikeyi while glorifying Kaushalya. Further, Manthara convinced the Queen that if Rama ascended to the throne, she would become a maid-servant of Kaushalya and live a life of misery.

Sorely afflicted by the arrow of Manthara's evil intent, Kaikeyi begged the maid-servant to help her upset the plans for Rama's coronation. Manthara then reminded Kaikeyi that the King had once offered to fulfill any two boons of her choice, and suggested that this was the perfect time to make her two requests: first, that Bharata be coronated instead of his brother, and second, that Rama be banished into the forest for fourteen years. By these two boons, said Manthara, Kaushalya would be deprived of all the joy she was expecting the next day at Rama's coronation.

Manthara further suggested that Kaikeyi retire that very night to the *kopa griha*, or the "sulking room" that queens entered in ancient times to bring some dissatisfaction or grievance to the attention of the king. Hearing that she had entered that room afflicted by some problem, Dasharatha would quickly come to see her and try to ease the difficulty. Eager to please her, he would surely pledge to grant any boon that she requested. At that time, after the King had taken an oath in the name of Rama to grant any boons, Kaikeyi would make her request.

According to plan, the King came to Kaikeyi's palace, eager to inform her about the coronation that was to take place the next day. He was sure that she would be as delighted as everyone else in the realm. To his surprise, however, he was informed that she had thrown herself in despair into the sulking room. He hurried to the side of his beloved Queen and then tried to find out the cause of her grief. When she indicated that granting her the two promised boons would bring her back to normalcy, he readily pledged to do so.

At that moment, Kaikeyi made her request for Bharata to become successor to the throne and Rama to be banished to the forest in the garb of an ascetic for a period of fourteen years. Hearing those burning words of Kaikeyi, the King was shocked and he became speechless.

Dasharatha pleaded with Kaikeyi and promised to recall Bharata to the kingdom and crown him as king, even though he was slightly younger than Rama. Then, he tried to convince her that Rama should not go to the forest because he could not bear that separation from his son. However, Kaikeyi taunted her husband and would not be moved from her resolve. Seeing the hopelessness of the situation, the King was immersed in grief. He knew that he could not break his promise to Kaikeyi without sacrificing his honor as a king, yet he was shattered and heartbroken at the prospect of losing Rama from his sight.

When morning came, Rama was summoned to the palace and he found his father lying on the floor as if enshrouded by death. Kaikeyi told Rama about the boons she had requested and explained that the King was torn between his intense affection for Rama and his honorable duty to grant those boons as promised. Thus, she suggested, Rama should relieve his father of his suffering and simply renounce the throne and quickly remove himself to the forest.

Due to his enlightened consciousness, Rama cheerfully and without hesitation agreed to Kaikeyi's request. Before the eyes of his grief-stricken relatives and the citizens of the kingdom, he left for the forest accompanied by his wife Sita and brother Lakshmana.

In the Divine plan the destructive jealousy of Manthara and Kaikeya was an instrument for the greatest good, for it brought Rama into the forest to fight the demons it was his destiny to conquer. However, in the practical life of Ayodhya its effects were devastating: a coronation turned into a banishment, the joyous songs of thousands of citizens of Ayodhya turned into sorrowful lamentations, and a close-knit royal family was torn apart, leading to the pathetic death of the distraught King Dasharatha himself.

The fact that a negative quality can be helpful from the Divine perspective does not imply that you should start helping God by becoming negative. It is your duty to yourself to strive at all times to overcome the negative within. If you encourage your impuri-

ties, as Kaikeyi did, then God uses you as a demoniac instrument in the Divine plan. But if you become a saintly personality, God makes you a tool of a sublime nature.

While striving to overcome the negative within yourself, however, do not become bitter about the negativity that abounds in others. Those negative qualities are there to urge you to become saintly, to foster and strengthen positive qualities. If the thorns were not present on the rose bush, the bush would not be able to bring forth beautiful flowers. So too, people who are afflicted with jealousy and hate, and who, without any reason, put obstacles on your path, are important aids in your spiritual evolution.

Possessing this understanding should not prevent you from doing everything possible to avoid being harmed by others. But when you can't avoid such harm, understand that it has a purpose and endure it. Such endurance becomes a powerful austerity on the spiritual path.

Insights into Removing Jealousy

It is necessary to understand the root cause of jealousy in order to eradicate it. Jealousy is a complex mental process that arises in a mind that has been degraded due to wastage of willpower. At the surface, you think that external objects, or persons are responsible for arousing jealousy in your heart.

But it is not so. You are afflicted with jealousy because you are dissatisfied with yourself and are not living a life of profoundity and enrichment. All of this inner unrest renders your mind amenable to psychological diseases—and jealousy is one of them.

Chronic jealousy cannot be overcome by mere words or mere theoretical understanding because it is a persistent opponent. The predicament of a jealous mind is similar to what happens when you put a little water in boiling milk: the moment you sprinkle the water, the milk settles down; however, as soon as you turn your back it is boiling over again. Much in the same way, every now and then your jealous mind calms down and you think, "What's the harm. Let those people I resent exist, happy and prosperous." But then, before you know it, jealousy comes frothing and bubbling up again as vigorous as ever!

Envy Is Based upon Illusion

In most cases, jealousy is based completely on illusion. What you think to be true of another person's situation is usually just not true. For example, one woman may see another woman with delicate skin walking very slowly and then stopping to have her shoes adjusted by the servant walking by her side. The mind of the observer may begin to burn with jealousy and she may feel, "She walks with such dignity. She looks so much fairer and more delicate than I do. She must be very prosperous to have a servant attend upon her every need so she doesn't have to do anything at all!" However, in truth the woman is walking slowly because she is crippled; her skin is fair because she is terribly anemic; and she must have an attendant put on her shoes because she has so much pain in her spine that she cannot even bend down!

If the jealous woman understood how things really were, she would laugh at her folly. What could she possibly be jealous about? Similarly, everything about which you develop jealousy is an expression of illusion. When you become jealous towards others, you are involving your mind in a process of imagination—not confronting reality.

The idea that other people are so happy and that you are miserable is wrong. Everyone is placed in a relative world. In the Divine creation, everyone who is not enlightened suffers from internal sorrow and restlessness. Everyone has his own problems and shortcomings. If you really knew the actual conditions of the people around you, you would develop a sense of sympathy and good will towards them, rather than jealousy.

If one of the suffering patients in a hospital is given breakfast in a nice manner and another suffering patient is not, there is nothing for the second patient to be really jealous about. Similarly, all who are caught in this world process are in a state of misery. Why should people be jealous of small advantages that others seem to have over them?

The Cosmic Perspective | To overcome jealousy, try to adopt a more advanced philosophical perspective. Begin to see yourself as a cosmic being, not as an individual, and all personalities as manifestations of the same Self.

Learn to see every human being as you would see your child or another near and dear relative. As such, they are all deserving of great joy. The happiness of all beings is yours. The world is your family, your own limb, your own Self. In the vast treasury of bliss that your inner Self enjoys, there is an abundance for all, and more is eternally forthcoming.

Your nose will not be jealous of your eyes because the eyes are spherical and the nose is conical. Each part of the body performs its function in relation to the organic unity of the whole. Much in the same way, every person is related to the organic whole of the universe and has a unique karmic role to play within it.

In the Divine Plan, no one can come in your way. To an untrained observer, the stars in the sky seem to be clustered together, as if they could bump into each other and get into each other's way. But an astronomer knows that each star is so many light years away from the others that they could never collide. Much in the same way, when you see a person threatening your progress, you must realize he is not in your way. No one can obstruct you; you are as free and separate as the distant stars. You are basically the Spirit and your freedom is endless.

You are shaping your destiny according to your own thoughts and actions, and therefore, no one is to be considered an impediment in your path. So instead of weakening your will by sustaining the fumes of jealousy in your heart, you should try to promote self-effort to better your circumstances.

The Role Of Karma You must realize that it is not other individuals but your own karma that governs your movement in life. If your karmic process entitles you to security, then even in catastrophic situations you will remain untouched, unaffected. On the other hand, if karma is not favorable, then even in the best situation or under the most favorable circumstances, you will slip on a banana peel and break your leg.

Any situation which invokes jealousy in you has come about on the basis of a karmic process. You must endure that situation, while at the same time continuing to affirm the goodness within yourself.

By maintaining jealousy towards any person, you are karmically drawing that person to yourself. When you are jealous you are constantly thinking of a certain person, linking your karmic process with that person's karmic process. In the course of repeated embodiments, one day you will draw that person to yourself as a close relative—perhaps as a brother, sister, child or any dear relative! At that time Nature will compel you to love that person unconditionally, overlooking any deficiencies in his or her personality.

Serve the Divine Self in Others | Try to seek out the Self in the person towards whom you become jealous—to reach out to and serve the higher aspect of the person. In other words, if you feel jealous towards a person, serve that person. Do not try to pull his legs or suppress him. When you try to supress a person towards whom you are jealous, you degrade both yourself and the person towards whom jealousy is directed. But by serving the person, you raise your nobler sentiments and eventually realize that you had no reason to be jealous at all.

Develop a spirit of charity and magnanimity to overcome jealousy. When you see a person more prosperous than you, feel delighted as if he were your own brother or dear friend. In the light of Yoga philosophy all beings are linked to the universal ocean of life; all human beings are children of the Divine Self. By developing joyousness towards the prosperity of others, you will be able to deck your personality with the flowers of divine virtues.

When you hear of the great achievements made by others, do not allow a burning sensation in your heart. Rather, become aware of the fact that what others have done you also can do. Great souls are only confirming your inner possibilities. Why should you frown at their greatness? Why should you look for their defects and talk about them?

Look for positive qualities in others, and try to emulate them. You are endowed with limitless possibilities. Try to direct your mind towards the unfoldment of your own latent talents and towards the enrichment of your personality.

If you eradicate jealousy from your heart, you will experience immense freedom and power of life. You will be an embodiment of love and compassion; and all your activities will promote peace and harmony in the world.

Therefore, strive to overcome your ego and develop magnanimity of heart. You should be inspired by people who are successful, and try to follow their example. Instead of jealousy, develop "zealousy!" Develop zeal to evolve, zeal to become a saintly personality, zeal to attain enlightenment—wherein all negative qualities disappear forever.

EXPLORING THE
ROOTS OF IMPURITY

To understand the *shad-ripus* more profoundly, one must look into their roots. The *shad-ripus* themselves are the ramifications of *mala*, or gross impurities of the conscious mind which derive their nutrition from subtle impressions of the unconscious. These subtle impressions cause distraction or agitation, known as *vikshepa*. In turn, these subtle impressions have as their ultimate root *avidya* or ignorance, also referred to as *avarana*, or mystic veiling of one's essential Divine nature.

Sediments of the Unconscious

Year after year, the vast ocean brings sediments to its depths, and these sediments turn into rocks. In the same way, the mind through waves of diverse functions, brings to its subconscious depths layers and layers of sediments which go to form subconscious obstructions in the manifestation of the Spirit and its energy.

As thought waves and desires rise and fall day by day, you gain experiences. Those experiences lead to the formation of subtle impressions or *samskaras* which abide in the unconscious, in the profound depths of one's being. They cannot be easily brought to the conscious purview, and yet they continue to exert their influence in one's daily life. From the depths of the unconscious, from time to time, there matures a group of impressions, and the thought-waves bring these impressions to the shore of normal consciousness. In other words, now and then there is an emergence of the unconscious contents in life's movements.

What is generally spoken of as the fructification of karmas in one's life is nothing but the emergence of the matured impressions from the unconscious which take over the realities of one's day to day life, and force one to pass through diverse experiences of pleasure and pain.

Human personality is a mold prepared by the mind, which continues to fashion it, to change it, to modify it. All events in life, all developments in circumstances, all associations and opportunities are explained in the terms of the workings of the subconscious impressions. Yoga does not consider the events of life as mere accidents.

It is not just the physical facts of your life but even your circumstances which are fashioned by the karmas or actions of your past. Yoga not only explains your physical diseases as expressions of your mental ailments, but also your circumstantial adversities as expressions of the contents of your unconscious.

However, this does not place you in the hands of a blind destiny, but rather it gives you a vision of freedom in life. No matter how much the past has built its sediments in the subconscious and the unconscious, it is you who have the power to modify and reconstruct the contents of your subconscious. You have fashioned your past, you are fashioning your present, and you are the architect of your future.

Thus, in brief, from the unconscious impressions there arise the subconscious desires or *vasanas.* These subconscious desires express themselves in the form of inclinations and urges in day-to-day life. What we call complexes in the mind mostly refer to these subconscious desires of the mind, which express themselves in the form of thought-waves or *vrittis.*

You can observe your mind. You can see how diverse thought waves arise from the unknown regions of your mind, and continue to float in your conscious mind as merry ripples. But soon these tiny ripples come into contact with the functions of imagination, misconception and egoistic interest. Then they turn into conscious desires.

When there is a vexing desire, the mirror of the mind becomes clouded. As a result you do not perceive your Self, you do not feel the depths of your being, wherein lie peace and bliss in abundance. It is through the imagination of the mind that you impose your own intrinsic joy on the objects outside of you, and then due to ignorance, you feel that it was the object that gave you happiness.

When a desire is not fulfilled it turns into craving. Cravings, desires and mental confusions continue to form diverse impressions in the subconscious, and from the subconscious, the sediments of experiences, the subtle *samskaras*, continue to deposit themselves in the unconscious depths of one's being. Thus the cycle of the mind continues revolving. With it continue the realities of one's day-to-day

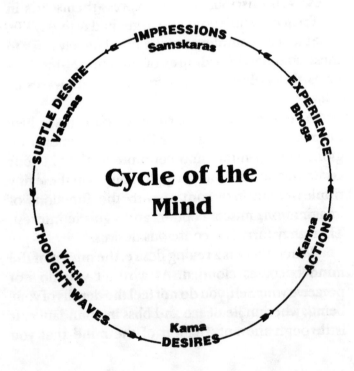

life, the stories of pleasure and pain, the dramas of comedy and tragedy.

The Kleshas or Mental Afflictions

According to Raja Yoga, there are five *kleshas* or afflictions which exist in the form of subtle impressions in the subconscious and unconscious mind. These are *avidya* (ignorance), *asmita* (egoism), *raga* (attachment towards objects that seem to give pleasure), *dwesha* (aversion or hatred towards objects that seem to give pain), and *abhinivesha* (clinging to life or dread of death). These *kleshas* govern the life of man by injecting their venom in mind's functions.

Human life is an elaboration of the subconscious and the unconscious contents. When the impressions of afflictions exist in the depth of one's being, his life expresses various forms of erroneous movements, mental eccentricities, physical maladies, and circumstantial adversities.

These *kleshas* are the basic roots for the development of any evil quality in one's personality. Therefore, in order to overcome any of the evils fully, those basic roots must be removed. Removal of the *kleshas* and attainment of Self-realization is, thus, the ultimate remedy for eradicating all that is negative in one's personality. Yoga aims at reducing and sublimating these subtle impressions and freeing the *chitta* or mind-stuff from all afflictions that distort the perception of the Reality of the Self.

Avidya
(Ignorance)

The most subtle and deep-rooted of the afflictions is *avidya* or ignorance. When the intellect is impure and its luminosity is clouded, one loses the glimpse of one's innate, essential universality and becomes identified with the ego-center. It is as if the sun comes to believe it is only the reflection of itself in a puddle, or the ocean believes it is only a wave, or a patch of blue has forgotten that it is the sky. This error is called ignorance or *avidya*. It is like a veil that covers the reality of the Self, and shows the ego to be the all important entity in life.

Ignorance consists in considering that which is not-self as the Self. Ignorance is a strange confusion of matter and spirit. The spirit is eternal, but due to ignorance you view the spirit within you as dependent on body, mind and intellect. You have forgotten, so to speak, that your real identity, your essential nature, is the immortal and eternal *Brahman*, the Absolute Self.

Asmita
(Ego)

Avidya gives rise to a sense of ego, a sense of individuality. Actually, the term ego is used in two senses, pure and impure. Pure ego is good and auspicious because it is characterized by humility and surrender to God, and it is in union with the Supreme Self.

But impure ego is colored, restricted and disfigured by the limitations of the mind, giving rise to the illusion that "This is me; these things are mine." The impressions of the defective egoistic functions go to form *asmita klesha*—the affliction of egoism—which is a very deep-rooted malady. The presence of *asmita klesha* is a result of identification with the body, mind and limited personality, rather than with one's own true identity, which is *Brahman* the Absolute.

Raga-Dwesha (Attachment-Hatred) *Asmita* becomes the basis of *raga* and *dwesha*—attachment and hatred. The human mind is attracted to things that are pleasant and repulsed by things that are painful. Thus, when pleasant objects are encountered or when pleasant conditions arise you develop a feeling, "May I have this object or condition more and more." The subtle impressions of this feeling go deep into the subconscious and unconscious mind and give rise to the affliction of attachment, or *raga klesha*.

On the other hand, when an object, person, or a circumstance is uncomfortable, or when it threatens your security and happiness, you wish to remove it, as one would remove a thorn from his tender foot. A sustained attitude of repulsion casts into the unconscious a subtle stream of the impressions of aversion. These go to form *dwesha klesha* or the affliction of hatred.

Human life witnesses alternating currents of love and hate, intense affection leading to mutual interdependence and gross identification, kindling hatred leading to a sustained animosity and deep-rooted aversion.

Attachment and hatred are the powerful forces that keep one's mental life agitated. When mental life is disturbed and the depths of the mind are filled with the impressions of like and dislike, one is not able to draw spiritual energy from the Self within.

The impressions of *raga* amd *dwesha* are the cause of all the miseries that arise in human life. They force one to create selfish karmas and these karmas lead one to embodiment or incarnation into the physical body with an individualized consciousness. You would not get into new embodiments if you did not have attachment and hatred. The presence of these emotions mean your mind is not at rest, your desires have not been fulfilled. Therefore, you have to come back again and again to fulfill them.

Abhinivesha
(Fear of Death)

Entering into embodiment brings with it fear of losing that embodiment. So *raga-dwesha* becomes the basis for the next affliction called *abhinivesha*—clinging to life and fear of death. To most people, the idea of losing one's life, of death to the physical body, seems like a total loss, complete darkness. No matter how much one might have read about the immortality of the soul and the illusion of the body, the fear of death strikes hard because it is deep-rooted and instinctive.

How Can the Kleshas Be Eradicated?

Consciously you can't directly attack the impressions of *avidya* or ignorance abiding in the deep unconscious. However, all your profound spiritual practices create new and powerful impressions which reduce the pressure of ignorance and make it easier for your intellect to confront a more accessible affliction: ego or *asmita klesha* along with its inseparable companions, *raga* and *dwesha*.

Although egoism is a more direct target than ignorance, it still is a very slippery opponent. It requires great discipline to make your ego your target. If you stare directly into the eyes of the ego, it shrivels, shrinks, disappears. However it is easier to listen to ego than to stare into its eyes.

An aspirant must realize that ego is a strong and enduring adversary with great mesmerizing powers. Although one must work tirelessly to outwit and reduce ego, one must understand that it cannot be conquered once and for all in a day. You can get away from ego temporarily by the practice of humility and other Divine virtues, but it will assert again whenever you relax your *sadhana*. This should not baffle you. Even anger, hate, irritability, jealousy—which are lesser enemies than ego itself—come back again and again to haunt an aspirant.

When one succeeds in bringing a high degree of integration in his personality, the *kleshas* become thinned out or attenuated. Subtle seeds of ignorance, egoism, attachment, hatred, and identification with the body continue to exist; but in expression, the life of the aspirant is decked with excellent virtues of the head and the heart. However, if he were to stop his mystic practices of meditation and enquiry, these seeds will manifest again in the form of gross afflictions, and many of his virtues will vanish, giving rise to negative qualities he never imagined he would have to confront.

The *kleshas* can be truly overcome only when one has become established in *samadhi* (superconsciousness), and one enjoys the sense of universality that results from this profound experience. Until that time, patience, faith and persistence are an aspirant's best weapons against the *kleshas*.

There is a wonderful story in the *Ramayana* that conveys in a most unforgettable manner the slippery nature of the ego, and the stubborn persistance of the seeds of the *kleshas* in the mind of even the most advanced aspirant. It is the story about Sage Narada and a powerful lesson taught to him by Lord Vishnu.

The Monkey Face

Once Sage Narada practised deep meditation in a beautiful cave near the Ganges River. His austerity was so intense that Indra, the celestial Lord of Gods, became concerned that Narada might try to claim his throne by the force of his austerity. So Indra sent Kama Deva, the cupid god, with his whole army to present temptations before the Sage and thus disturb his practice of austerity.

Accordingly, Kama Deva, with his retinue of celestial attendants, went to Narada's cave. Soon the flowers burst into beauteous blossoms and the soft breeze began to blow, and the *apsaras* (celestial nymphs) began to sing and dance. Kama Deva, along with his attendants, exercised all their powers of allurement against the mind of Narada, but the Sage remained unperturbed. When Narada could not be shaken, Kama Deva became afraid of the Sage, thinking that he might destroy him by his fierce look. When Kama Deva fell at Narada's feet seeking his forgiveness, Narada simply smiled and said that he held no grudge against him, for he was merely doing his duty.

As a result of this experience, however, Narada developed a subtle pride. He thought to himself, "I have conquered Kama. I have excelled many sages and saints who could not prevail against the celestial temptations." With that sense of pride swelling within his heart, he went to Lord Shiva and related all that had happened.

Lord Shiva smiled and said, "O Narada, you are a devotee of Lord Vishnu. By His Grace nothing is impossible for you. However, please do not relate this experience of yours to Lord Vishnu."

Sri Narada then went to Brahma, the creator, and told him how he had defeated Kama. Lord Brahma praised him and also advised him not to relate his experience to Lord Vishnu. However, Narada did not heed to his advice, and hastened to Vaikuntha, where Lord Vishnu dwells.

Lord Vishnu welcomed the Sage and asked, "O Sage, I have not seen you for a long time. Where have you been?" Sri Narada then told everything about his confrontation with Kama, and concluded saying, "O Lord, it was all by Your grace that I accomplished this most difficult task, a task in which even great sages of yore had failed." Lord Vishnu smiled and said, "Nothing is impossible for you, O Sage. Kama is no match for you!" But realizing that Narada had developed pride and was falling prey to spiritual delusion, Lord Vishnu decided to cure him of his malady.

Departing from Lord Vishnu, the Sage resumed his normal habits of travelling through the various *lokas* or worlds. Soon he passed through a kingdom which he had never seen before, a kingdom in which all men and women were exceedingly handsome.

The ruler of that kingdom was King Sheelanidhi, and he had a beautiful daughter named Shrimati. The time had arrived for the lovely Princess to choose a suitable husband for herself, and for that purpose her father had arranged a *swayambara*. According to this method of marriage, many eligible princes were invited to present themselves before the Princess, who would then evaluate each suitor and place her garland on the one she chose to be her husband.

Curious to find out more about this kingdom, Sri Narada went to the palace and introduced himself to King Sheela-nidhi. The King was delighted to have the company of the Sage, and asked him to give blessings to his daughter and fortell her future.

When Narada looked into the astrological conditions of the Princess and examined her palm, he realized that whoever married her would become the greatest person in the world. He thought within himself, "Why shouldn't I become the blessed suitor of this glorious Princess and attain supreme greatness?" However, hiding his feelings, he simply told the King that his daughter was endowed with excellent qualities, and then gave his blessings to her.

After seeing the Princess, Narada could not rest in peace. He thought to himself, "How am I to marry her? My austerity-torn body is thin and emaciated, and the Princess would not be attracted to me." Soon an idea entered his mind, and Narada invoked the presence of Lord Vishnu, his best friend and benefactor, who would surely help him secure the hand of the Princess.

When Lord Vishnu appeared before him shining in His Divine Glory, Sage Narada said, "O Lord, You are the giver of all desires. I desire to marry Shrimati, the daughter of King Sheela-nidhi. For this purpose I want to have a body just like Yours, because it is only through such beauty that I could secure the Princess for myself." Lord Vishnu smiled at the power of His own *maya* (cosmic illusion), which had degraded the mind of the Sage to such an extent, and said, "O Sage, I will do all that is good for you." Thus saying, Lord Vishnu disappeared.

In a moment, Narada looked at himself and found his rugged body had been transformed into the body of Lord Vishnu! With eager anticipation, he hastened his steps to the *swayambara* hall where kings and princes from many different lands had assembled, each desiring to win the hand of Princess Shrimati. Narada then took a formost seat so that the Princess was sure to behold his beauty.

At the proper time, the Princess entered the Hall with a garland in her hands, her eyes moving eagerly in all directions in order to choose a husband. As she looked towards Narada she immediately recoiled from him and turned away. Thinking that perhaps she had missed seeing him, Narada moved to another seat closer to the Princess. But the Princess again turned away from him. Narada eagerly moved from one seat to another, and the Princess continued to avoid him.

At that time there were two messengers of Lord Shiva *(Shiva-ganas)* who were amused at the strange behavior of the Sage. Giggling with amusement, they whispered into his ears, "O Sage, why don't you go and look at your face in that nearby pool of water?" Out of curiosity, Narada went over to the pool and looked at himself. To his horror and frustration he saw that he had the hideous face of a monkey. Though his body was beautiful, this hideous face had created such a strange contrast that he had become a ridiculous figure.

All his dreams of glory and greatness were shattered to pieces. His mind became so filled with wrath that he turned to Shiva's attendants and pronounced a curse: "You wretched souls! You who have laughed at my distress, may you incarnate as demons and suffer untold miseries at the hands of monkeys!"

Then, all of a sudden, a dazzling figure entered the hall. It was Lord Vishnu Himself, and the Princess readily offered the garland to Him. As the couple was departing in a celestial chariot, Lord

Vishnu stopped before the Sage and asked, "O Sage, why are you so troubled? May I be of some help to you?" At this Narada became doubly incensed and said, "You, Lord Hari, since there is no one greater than yourself who can constrain you, you continue to play tricks on your devotees and delight at their misery. Today I am going to teach you a lesson. I am pronouncing a curse on you: May you incarnate as a human being, and may you pine for the Princess for whom you gave me a monkey face. Further, because of my monkey face, it is the monkeys who will be your friends in this miserable predicament."

Lord Vishnu said with humility, "O Sage, I accept your curse. I will incarnate as Rama. The messengers of Shiva, according to your curse, will incarnate as demons. This Princess, who is none other than Lakshmi, the Goddess of Prosperity, will incarnate as Sita. As Rama, I will experience untold sufferings because of my separation from Sita. I will befriend monkeys, who will form an army to help me destroy the demons, whose spirits then will be restored to their former status of being Shiva's messengers. Then, once again, I will be united with Sita. All this is the Divine Plan which will come to pass."

At these words of Lord Vishnu, the inner eye of Narada was opened. As if awakened from a dream, Narada fell at the feet of Lord Vishnu, pleading, "O Lord, render my curse void. I know I was deluded by *avidya*. Please do not let this aspect of Your *maya* delude my mind again. O Lord, I seek refuge in You."

Lord Vishnu lifted up the Sage and conforted him. He told Sri Narada that he should not grieve, that the stream of devotion would ever flow in his heart, and that he would not be overpowered by delusion anymore!

On the spiritual path, in order to overcome the deep-rooted *kleshas* or mental afflictions, an aspirant must bring about the perfect integration of his entire personality—a total internal transformation, not just superficial changes. As this process unfolds, some parts of the personality more readily become Divine, yet others remain unchanged—like the face of a monkey! As long as there is a monkey face, liberation—like Goddess Lakshmi in this story—cannot be won, but will continue to turn its face away.

Clearly, Narada's proud assertion that he had conquered *kama* was premature. Lord Vishnu readily saw how desire, anger, greed and pride still lingered in Narada's mind, and how readily he would fall prey to delusion. So He used His *maya* to bring all this impurity to the surface. His Divine scheme was not an act of cruelty, but a profoundly compassionate way of teaching His devotee that more austerity was needed.

Whenever there is supressed evil in a person, the Divine plan works in mysterious ways to reveal what is hidden and remove it. When a surgeon learns that his patient has a tumor, he quickly applies his knife and cuts it out. Similarly, when God finds a spiritual tumor within your soul, it must be removed—no matter what it takes. Initially, as a result of this Divine surgery, you may feel humiliated, However, as you tide over your apparent adversity and see your weaknesses disappear, you will find yourself much stronger and more enriched than before. Whenever God seems to frustrate the desires of a devotee, behind the scenes is His loving hand, ever intent upon leading the devotee from darkness to light.

Destroying the Seeds of Afflictions

When a Yogi truly succeeds in freeing his reason from the burden of all afflictions, his intellect becomes intuitive. The intuitive intellect tears the veil of ignorance. All the seeds of afflictions are burned up. They can no longer envenom the mind. They can no longer obscure life's innermost expansion. They can no longer restrict and pervert the universal harmony that vibrates through all life. This is the burned-up state or *dagdha* state of afflictions which is to be acquired as the goal of all Yogic practices.

When this state has been reached, the Yogi enjoys life in its fullness. He expresses this fullness of experience through a mind pulsating with dynamic and creative thoughts towards the promotion of harmony and peace in the world. He manifests this abundant experience through actions that waft the fragrance of his enlightenment, and through external circumstances which exist to express the beauty and majesty of life.

SECRETS OF
PURIFYING THE MIND

The majesty of the Divine Self shines through
this universe like a million suns, and to experience
this glory we have been given the gift of the medium
of the mind. However, impurities such desire, anger,
greed, pride, delusion and jealousy exist in the mind
like clouds, and with a clouded mind the sun of the
Self is obscured. What, then, should one do to
remove the clouds of mental impurity?

Be Patient and You will succeed!

In learning to handle any negative quality, do
not struggle too ferociously with it or become convinced that you are a failure whenever you notice its
presence within your mind. Never sit down and cry,
"I have been a Yogi for five years. And now look: I still
have fear, I still have jealousy, I still have so many
impurities in my mind. It will take too many years
and births to attain perfection!"

You must realize that because you are alive you
must feel many emotions. Spiritual movement is not

for the dead, it is for the living. If you do not feel jealousy at all in your heart, then there is no spiritual movement for you. If you do not feel fear at all, you are already dead. If you are never awakened to anger because of provocation, you are already too feeble to move a finger!

If you tread the path and find that your mind is not as pure as you wish it to be, don't worry. You must realize that the movement is progressive. You should move on in spite of the negativity in the mind.

Learn to observe the mind and see what emotions are there. Feel you are an alert, objective witness, watching the clouds as they form and dissolve. Your negative emotions are all awakening your inner aspiration. They have a role; they have their purpose.

However, at the same time, be careful. You must move on without justifying those negative qualities within you. Although it is pointless to struggle viciously with mental impurities, meaningful self-effort must be employed to control and gradually eliminate them.

In this process, try to see that impure thoughts and feelings are not allowed to find expression in the realm of speech and action. When you observe the rising of anger, for example, in the plane of thought, try to contain it, to nip it at the bud. Once you begin to express words out of anger, the situation gets out of hand. Words create their own problems. If you allow things to go further, and by your action try to hurt others, you have really initiated a potentially devastating chain reaction.

Promote Sattwa and
Soften the "Lines" of Impurity

As we have seen, the three *gunas*—*sattwa* (purity or harmony), *rajas* (restlessness or externalization), and *tamas* (negativity and dullness)—play a critical role in the matter of mental impurity. When *tamas* predominates, impurities in the mind become demoniac and gross. The *tamasic* form of an impurity is like tar—you can't rub it off easily.

Or thought of in another way, *tamasic* impurities endure like lines chiseled in rock. Even after a hundred years they are still there. When the mind is *rajasic*, the impurities are like lines drawn on clay. You can mold them and change them easily. When the mind is *satwic*, the impurities are like lines drawn on water. They are there one moment like gentle ripples and then gone the next. Therefore, the *satwic* mind must be promoted with great patience so that impurities can be eliminated.

Accentuate the Positive to
Eliminate the Negative

In a world full of stress and tension, due to lack of *satsanga* (good association), the human mind clings to negative feelings. Out of all the feelings that are generated day by day, the negative feelings born of *rajas* and *tamas* become more abounding. But that should not be. The negative should not stay in your mind.

In Chapter 17 of *Srimad Bhagavad Gita*, Lord Krishna gives a powerful teaching about promoting a joyous and *satwic* mind through the practice of a unique form of mental austerity that includes four powerful techniques: *manah prasadah, saumyatwam, maunam, atma-vinigraha*, and *bhava samshudhi*.

Manah Prasadah (Joyousness) ‖ The first aspect of austerity of the mind is *manah prasadah*—allowing the mind to be joyous. People who have been accustomed to considering austerity as something harsh will be surprised that promoting joyousness can be thought of as austerity. In Yoga philosophy, austerity is not supposed to give you pain, but discipline you so that the spirit flows in a healthy, unobstructed way through your personality. Thus, the effort to maintain cheerfulness of the mind is a dynamic aspect of austerity.

Many people have developed the habit of allowing their minds to become negative. You must watch your own mind very carefully. Try to develop the philosophy that the world is an expression of Divine creation. There is intelligence and a guiding purpose behind the world; you have nothing to worry about. There should be no room for grief, dejection, and sorrow in your life.

Always think of the positive things that you have acquired and accomplished. By thinking of the blessings God has given you, you will have so many reasons for being serene and cheerful. More than anything else, understand that the Divine hand is sustaining your personality at every moment. The awareness that Divinity is within you will fill your mind with joy.

By adopting this philosophy of loving God at all times, you allow your mind to be serene and joyous. Do not develop negative thoughts. When they do arise, simply be a witness to them.

When you keep your mind in a negative state, you will be steadily generating negative impressions, and your mind will be forced to stay negative by the weight of these impressions. Due to the weight of the impressions of sadness and sorrow, you will not be happy even when you find yourself in a wonderful situation, a situation you have been craving for a long time.

Your experiences of joy and sorrow are intimately related to the impressions of your unconscious. Therefore, it is an important part of austerity not to let your mind be negative. Let your spirit soar high, and let your mind be joyous.

Saumyatwam
(Gentleness)

The next aspect of mental austerity is *saumyatwam* (gentleness). When you confront a situation that provokes your mind into becoming agitated or negative, simply look at it without building up ill will towards anyone. Let your mind stay gentle, composed, and detached. You will discover an amazing spiritual strength within yourself.

By reacting to external situations, you allow your mind to become agitated. An agitated mind creates negative impressions in your unconscious. Gradually a habit builds up. Your mind constantly reacts to things no matter how they are. If you are looking for absolute perfection according to the concepts of your ego, you will never find it; there will always be something to irritate your mind.

If you are vulnerable to negative influences, or if you have already created in your mind a habit of reacting to everything, then all you need is just a pretext. A leaf might fall on your head, and it would be enough to put you into a state of agitation!

Saumyatwam implies that the mind becomes serene, calm, and unaffected—just like the face of Buddha. When you watch a movie, you are always aware of the fact that all the happenings on the screen are mere appearances. Therefore, though you feel sorrow at the tragic developments, you are not deeply affected in your heart. Similarly, be a spectator to your mind and its changes, knowing that faith in God will ultimately make you truly gentle.

Maunam (Silence)

The next practice relating to the mind is *maunam* (silence). If you watch your mind, you will notice that a great many thoughts enter it constantly—so many, in fact, that after a while, it is as if a lively discussion is going on deep in your mind. The world may be quiet around you, yet your mind might be as noisy as a market-place. This should not be so.

When you are engaged in various actions, watch your mind. Do not entertain conflicting thoughts and do not allow the mind to be agitated. You should be like a swan. A swan enters the lake and sports with the water, but the moment the sport is over the swan shakes off the water particles and flies away. Much in the same manner, perform your duties well in the world, but the moment you retire, shake off all your tensions and worries and relax in the arms of God, in the arms of Divinity within.

The thoughts of the mind should be as still as a lake without waves. You can do this by turning your mind to God and practising *japa* (repetition of Divine name). Mentally repeat the name as you allow the feeling of Divine Presence to enfold you. Gradually your mind will become calm and quiet.

Observing silence of speech for an hour or two in daily life—called *mauna vrata* (the vow of silence)—is also conducive to the mental austerity of *mauna*.

Atma-Vinigraha (Mastery over the Senses)

The next austerity of the mind is *atma-vinigraha*, which means mastery over the senses. It is the subtle desires of the mind that render the senses uncontrollable. Controlling the desires as they enter the mind becomes a fascinating austerity. Each time there is a mental whisper urging you to become a slave of the senses, try to brush that whisper aside. Assert your mastery over the senses and, thereby, mastery over every situation in life.

Bhava Samshudhi (Purity of Feeling) The next austerity of the mind is *bhava samshudhi*. *Bhava* means feeling. All human experiences are based upon the feelings that you have. Within families, within society, the feelings that exist between different people play a great role. The same human being that gives you great joy today can give you great sorrow tomorrow if the feeling changes. Therefore, you must learn to watch your feelings and observe the types of feelings you hold within your heart.

Develop the quality of grasping that which is positive in others so that your feeling is always magnanimous. Do not draw to yourself the negative qualities of others. If you have built up a bitter mind, each time you see other people, you will notice that everyone has a particular type of error or defect in their personality. You may even conclude, "This world is filled with useless people. What is going to happen to the world?"

You must understand how much you are hurting yourself when your mind continuously focuses on the negative in others. As time goes by you realize how much negativity you have stored in your unconscious. Why not change your attitude in such a way that you go on filtering out that which is best? Look at any person and realize that God is shining through his eyes, that the Divine *prana* (life-force) is pulsating through him.

All people make mistakes. However, despite those mistakes there is always something in everyone that you can admire. If, at the moment, you can perceive no such admirable quality in the other person, then just keep your mind detached. But do not go on looking for defects and keeping your mind filled with negative feeling.

One who is practising *bhava samshudhi* will enjoy reflecting on this parable based on the *Mahabharata* involving Duryodhana, who was the embodiment of all forms of impurity, and Yudhishthira, who was the embodiment of virtue. Once Guru Dronacharya created a special project for those two disciples. Duryodhana was asked to go out into the world and find the best person he could find, a person who was absolutely faultless. Yudhishthira was asked to find the worst person he could find, a person full of faults. After a while they both returned to present their findings.

Yudhishthira reported to Dronacharya that he could not find anyone other than himself who was so full of faults and had so many defects to overcome. Because he was introspective, he did not care about the faults of others; his mind was concerned with his own faults. His whole focus was on improving himself, and his righteousness did not allow him to judge others. Therefore, he brought that report to his Guru and Dronacharya was pleased.

Duryodhana, reporting the results of his research, said, "I could not find anyone, anywhere, who was absolutely perfect except myself. Even in you, Guru, I find many faults!" Needless to say, Dronacharya was not pleased with his arrogant disciple.

As the story leads us to understand, one must be tolerant of others' defects, but never of his own. By the practice of persistent introspection, learn to see your weaknesses and strive to overcome them. Develop compassion towards the weaknesses of others, but never justify your own.

It is much more important in spiritual movement to focus your attention on your own shortcomings. If you do there is a concrete, tangible advantage. On the other hand, if you focus your attention on finding mistakes in others, you have accomplished nothing. You have done no good to others, and merely crowded your own mind with negativity. It is a much better policy to look at the good qualities of others and thereby be inspired by what you see.

If you are truly practising austerity of the mind through the techniques of *manah prasadah, saumyatwam, maunam, atma-vinigraha,* and *bhava samshudhi,* the impurities of your personality will gradually be destroyed. The potentiality of your spirit will shine forth just as gold shines when it is melted. That is the purpose of austerity—to purify the unconscious, which will then enable you to enter into higher levels of spiritual experience.

Come Closer to God

The art of spiritual life consists in shortening the distance, so to speak, between yourself and the Divine Self. It is the art of coming closer to God until there is Absolute Union. In actuality, the Divine Self, who is the source of all forms of happiness, is nearer than your very heart, and yet that Self seems so far away. This is a great paradox.

When the mind is filled with anger, hate, greed and passion, the spirit in you turns away from the Divine Self, and a distance begins to grow between you and your innermost Self. But when the mind is filled with love, cheerfulness, contentment, and other Divine virtues, the distance is shortened. This is implied in the saying, "You take one step towards God and God takes one hundred steps towards you." When the mind shines with perfect purity, there is no distance at all. Through the clear mirror of mind you realize, "I am He!" and become free of the cycles of birth and death.

Detach and Attach

Sri Shankaracharya said: *"Satsangatwe nihasangatwam, nihasangatwe nirmohatwam, nirmohatwe nishchaltatwam, nischaltatwe jivanmuktih."*—*"Satsanga* leads you to detachment,

detachment destroys *moha* or delusion. Free of delusion, you become rooted in God within you, unaffected by the world. That state then leads to *jivanmukti* or liberation."

The concept of "detachment" is poorly understood by the majority of people. To most people the word implies becoming cold, indifferent. Nothing could be more incorrect. Philosophical detachment is quite the opposite. Detachment frees you from delusion, selfishness, bitterness and cruelty and fills you with the compassion and joy that are the qualities of your true inner Self.

In leading you to detachment, *satsanga* helps you to discover that the spirit within you is the same as the universal Spirit, the Self, and as such you are not dependent upon anything for your happiness. Through *satsanga* you break the chains of psychological dependence on people and objects and gain an internal sense of freedom. This form of detachment brings to one's personality a special integrity and sense of majesty that is the source of all that is truly wonderful in life.

A person who is dependent on the world, whose mind is complexed and filled with illusions, may have many wonderful, virtuous qualities; yet, there will be other areas of his personality that remain as rough and jagged as broken glass, and can be very destructive and hurtful to others. One who is bound to the world through attachments invariably experiences bitterness and hatred—in direct mathematical proportion to his attachments—towards anything that interferes with that attachment.

It is the deep-seated urge of every soul to affirm that the all-pervasive, all-encompassing Divine Self alone exists, that the world is filled to the brim with the existence of God and nothing else. With this affirmation, the soul becomes one with *Brahman* just as a patch of blue becomes one with the vast blue sky and a wave becomes one with the ocean. However, due to the limited and complexed mind, this longing for "attachment" to the Self becomes perverted into the degrading affliction of *raga* or attachment to the names and forms of the world.

Similarly, it is the deep-seated urge of the soul to negate all names and forms, all individualization, all sense of "I-ness and mine-ness." However, again due to limitations of mind, this longing to push away the entire illusory world of time and space becomes perverted into *dwesha klesha*, or the urge to be rid of select objects that bring pain to the ego. It is through *satsanga*, or association with those who are highly advanced, that an aspirant gradually learns to see *raga* and *dwesha* in the light of wisdom.

As you begin to practise the art of detachment, learn to notice what happens each time you become happy in a particular situation. You begin to listen to the subtle whispers of illusion and develop a desire, "May I have this situation, may I have the company of this particular person or particular object." At first the glue is not so strong, it doesn't stick much and you could have walked away from the object. But if your fascination lingers day by day, and you continue reminding yourself, "How wonderful! How wonderful!," the glue becomes strong. Eventually the glue becomes so strong that suddenly you realize you are stuck and can't get free even if you wanted to!

Don't let anything of this world stick to you. The objects are not reality. What should stick to you is the awareness that the Divine Self is the underlying reality of your existence. You should get more and more attached to God, and less and less attached to the objects of the world. To be glued to God, of course, implies understanding and becoming one with your own essential nature.

When the full moon casts a lovely reflection in a vessel of water, you look up from the small vessel to admire the real moon, the source of the reflection, shining in the sky. Similarly, each time a wonderful situation, object, or person comes to bring you joy, let your mind turn to the Divine Self, which is the source of that joy, beauty, and goodness. Your mind should not stop at the object, but go beyond. See God shining in everything and everyone just as you see the moon shining in different reservoirs of water. In this way, you break the illusion that binds you to objects as the source of your happiness.

Similarly, each time something painful presents itself, instead of feeling, "Let me remove that object, get rid of it, destroy it," learn to see the Divine plan urging you through the painful situation to become stronger and more enduring so that you can eventually go beyond the fragile ego and discover the imperishable, transcendental reality of your personality.

Your sense of individuality is only a reflection of the Absolute Self in the pool of the mental process—like the trembling reflection of the radiant full moon in a small pool of water. Like that trembling reflection that is ever disturbed by every fish, frog and breeze that blows, the reflected self in you is always dependent on the mind and its vicissitudes. Every little thing can shake that spirit within you and make it tremble. Through *satsanga*, you realize that you are actually the radiant full moon of the Self, no longer stuck in the predicament of abiding in a little pool of water, dependent upon everything that influences the water from morning to night. You are not confined to your body, you are not confined to a world of time and space. You are *Brahman* the Absolute.

Transform Your Personality
Through Integral Yoga

As time passes by, you continue to change your external habits, reactions, and values, but you are not transformed. You remain the same person with similar cravings and weaknesses, with similar defects such as irritability, greed, falsehood and infatuation. An aspirant should not perpetuate his same old personality. He must bring about a transformation in his inner nature. Spiritual understanding is like the philosopher's stone that converts the base metal of human desires into the shining gold of spiritual aspiration.

Integration of personality and transformation of your inner life—these are the most important aspects of your spiritual movement. You can accomplish them by following the path of Integral Yoga— the path wherein you blend all the important elements of the different Yogas in your daily life. In other words, there should be a blend of meditation *(dhyana)*, selfless action *(karma)*, devotion *(bhakti)*, and wisdom *(jnana)* in your daily life.

Gradually, you will outgrow your temptations, weaknesses, and illusions. You will no longer be like a crow feeding on vanity, but like a swan that soars in the boundless expansion of the Self, and sports in the lake of spiritual bliss.

Meditation (DhyanaYoga) Every day allow your mind to experience serenity through the practice of concentration and meditation. Relax your mind, give it space to soar beyond the stress of daily life. Although any form of meditation is valuable, devout meditation—meditation on God, with or without form, concrete or abstract—is the most powerful in the project of overcoming mental impurity. As you feel your personality enveloped by Divine Presence you will gain a new energy to overcome your defects and promote impressions of purity and peace within your heart. Silence the restless mind and withdraw the outgoing senses. Through the windows of serenity, you will glimpse the glorious vistas of universal consciousness, and the breeze of freedom blowing into your heart will quench all suffering.

Wisdom
(Jnana Yoga)

Enquire into "Who am I?" and discover the nature of the Self under the guidance of a spiritual teacher. Gain an insight into the fact that you are not this body, mind and senses. You are not this passing personality. The true Self in you is universal, all-pervading, one, and nondual. You are vast like the sky. So why should you be enchanted by the passing clouds of worldly glory? You are profound like the ocean. Why should you be constantly agitated by the frisking of the little fish of desire?

Listen, reflect and meditate. Assert your essential nature. Elevate your mind. Do not entertain thoughts that are degrading, desires that are humiliating, and concepts of life that are founded on ignorance.

You are the architect of your destiny. You are not an accidental product of material elements. Just as every wave has its identity in the ocean, and every patch of blue has its identity in the sky, your real identity is *Brahman* the Absolute. You are the ruler of your circumstances, the designer of your personality, and the molder of the world that you see around you. In fact, you are the only Reality.

*Selfless Service
(Karma Yoga)*

Selfless service is one of the most powerful and effective aids in the purification of mind. Through Karma Yoga, you allow your energies to be utilized in a dynamic way. When your energies are not well utilized, you are inclined to *tamas*—inertia, negativity and dullness. When you are *tamasic* your mind becomes like a transistor radio tuned to discordant music that emanates from so many other negative minds.

When you keep your mind involved in performing action that inspires and purifies, you rise beyond the negative sentiments that cloud your mind. You begin to realize that the things that created anger, hate, and jealousy in your heart mean nothing.

Karma Yoga is a process of spiritualizing all activity with the understanding that your entire life can become an artistic process leading to Self-realization. Imbued with this understanding, a Karma Yogi converts every aspect of his work into an act of meditation and prayer.

A Karma Yogi develops the attitude of renouncing or surrendering the fruit of action. Without looking for an egoistic reward or caring whether someone else is there to appreciate his actions, he performs his duties to the best of his ability with an internal sense of integrity. Although he makes the effort to be successful in every project, even if his actions do not yield the expected outcome, he will continue to perform his duties with patience. By not being attached to the fruits of action, he is able to stay balanced in gain and loss, and will not be heart-broken over the vicissitudes of life.

The human heart is constantly pressured by the urge to discover its oneness with the Divine Self through acts of goodness, kindness, generosity, self-effacing love and magnanimity. As a Karma Yogi, an aspirant cultivates this urge in order to attain mental purity and to move on to the heights of spiritual realization.

An aspirant must not let the vision of harmony and oneness be dissipated because of the illusions of give and take that sustain the practical realities of life. He must give with utter humility, and receive with a spirit of uplifting love proceeding from the Divine Self. His giving is an expression of his Divine love, and his receiving is an acceptance of a Divine blessing.

Acts of goodness must be like an aroma emanating from a blooming soul. You should not even be aware at the egoistic level of your acts of goodness done to others. An interesting story is told about a sage who, by the force of his austerities, deserved a heavenly boon. The angels insisted on giving the boon of miraculous powers to him, but he pleaded that the boon should rather be given to his shadow. As a result, the shadow of the Sage worked wonders in the world, while he himself remained oblivious of all the good that proceeded from him. This is the secret art of doing the utmost good to one and all.

Give abundantly, with love and humility. Be a dynamic servant of humanity. Share all that you have with others. Share your very being with all. Do not be miserly. Do not keep your knowledge, your wisdom, and your talents locked up in the confines of your own little self. Fling open the doors of your mind. Just as imprisoned air blends with the joyous breeze, so too allow yourself to blend with the breeze of cosmic life and be free.

Devotion
(Bhakti Yoga)

For Karma Yoga to be perfect, it should blend with devotion, or *bhakti*. As you pray to God and practise repetition of mantra and devout meditation, you develop an awareness of the sweetness of Divine Love and your mind gathers strength. When the stream of Divine Love begins to flow in your heart, it washes away all impurities, and the subtlest traces of anger, jealousy, hatred, and greed are eliminated.

Bhakti Yoga teaches you to offer your ego and mind and all your sentiments to God, and allow Divine Love to develop. Each time a negative sentiment asserts within your mind, offer it to God: "Oh Lord, the mind is Yours, the ego is Yours. This negative sentiment is here but I don't want it. I can't do anything about it at this moment; so I offer it all to You."

Bhakti Yoga also gives a new dimension to human love. As insight into Divine love grows, you realize that all human expressions of love are like sparks, while Divine love is the real fire. When you love God in every relationship, human love becomes profound.

Without love of God, your love for people remains shallow. That love is based on *moha* (delusion) and *raga* (attachment). It binds you to another person, yet never feels secure. However, if you have the understanding that God is the innermost source of love, and that Divine love is ever present and available within your heart, then you will always enjoy a state of fundamental security. Divine love does not come and go; it is always there as an inexhaustible fount of strength and sweetness.

Demons are Gods-in-the-Making

In the Indian scriptures like the *Mahabharata, Ramayana,* and *Devi Mahatmya,* mental impurities and afflictions are described as demons with personalities who battle against the gods and great incarnations. It is particularly interesting to note that when Rama destroys Ravana or Krishna destroys Shishupal, for example, there emerges from the demon a wonderful light which enters into the Divine being. How could it be that these terrible beings simply merge spontaneously with the Deity at the time of their death?

The fact is that Ravana, Shishupal, and all the other demons are nothing but "short-circuited" gods, just as anger, greed, jealousy and the other mental impurities are nothing but spiritual energy gone haywire.

When electricity is short-circuited, it becomes dangerous. Correct the short-circuit, and the energy flows in the right way. Similarly, the impurities within you are short circuits of your spiritual energy. When the Divine within you slays your demon impurities, the energy within them becomes spiritual.

What is anger? Nothing but love that has been obstructed. What is desire? Nothing but inner contentment that has been veiled. All negative qualities are obstructed views of the innately positive within you. The positive is your nature; the negative is the result of obstruction. When you are sick, the diseased state is not your nature. Your healthy state has become obstructed. Once this is remedied, health flows. Similarly, as you remedy the inner illness of ignorance, virtuous qualities begin to flow spontaneously.

Therefore, in Vedantic psychology, it doesn't matter when anger began, or what factors in your childhood encouraged it. The Vedantic psychologist—the Guru—reminds you that what matters is to understand that the impurity isn't really there. By enhancing the positive within yourself the negative will simply vanish.

From Impurity to Purity— The Story of Kaliya Daman

In ancient days when Lord Krishna was living in Vrindaban, everything was wonderful in that forest except for one thing: the Yamuna River was poisoned by a snake that dwelt in the subterranean level of the river. In a big hole in the bed of the river lived Kaliya, spewing forth venom from his numerous hoods. The water was so poisoned that as birds flew by they fell dead from the effect of the poison. So it became the task of Krishna to rid the Yamuna of Kaliya.

One day, as Krishna was playing with his friends, he deliberately let his ball fall into the river. Telling the others that he was going to recover the ball, Krishna climbed a great Kadamba tree which had a branch jutting toward the river and jumped right in.

To the dismay and shock of all who feared the dangerous snake, Krishna dove deep into the bed where Kaliya was sleeping. Kaliya woke up with anger and began to hiss through all his hoods and emit venom, but Krishna was unaffected. Then Kaliya entwined Krishna and the whole body of Kaliya rose above the water.

When people saw Krishna entwined they thought that he was going to be destroyed, and they started weeping and crying. Krishna then smiled, and in order to give comfort to them, he swelled up his body and Kaliya became uncomfortable and let go of him.

As soon as Krishna became free, he started to jump and dance upon Kaliya's hoods. As he did so, Kaliya began to emit jewels from each hood. As Krishna continued dancing joyously from hood to hood, Kaliya became exhausted. At that time the wives of Kaliya arose and prayed to Krishna saying,

"O Krishna, save our lord, our husband. Do not destroy him."

Kaliya himself then developed an understanding and love for Krishna and said, "How blessed am I that your sacred feet have danced on my hoods. I should not be destroyed." When Krishna realized that Kaliya had submitted himself to him and had earnestly and sincerely repented, Krishna then asked Kaliya to move away from the Yamuna River and go to live in the ocean. Kaliya did so, taking his family away to abide in the vast ocean. Vrindaban again became the perfect abode for all, with sweet water flowing in the Yamuna and Krishna playing on his flute.

In this story, Kaliya represents ego and the Yamuna River represents the *chitta* or mind-stuff that is dominated by ego. In the subterranean part of the river, or in the unconscious of your mind, there dwells ignorance, with its special expression in the form of ego. While that ego dwells in the unconscious, it goes on poisoning one's thoughts. If the *vrittis* (thought-waves) of the mind were freed of *asmita*—the ego sense—they would become nectarine. That is the goal of Yoga. But how does one drive the ego out? What should one do in order to purify the mind?

Begin by allowing Krishna's ball—that is to say, allow remembrance of God, good karmas, a bit of Divine grace—to enter into your unconscious, into your heart. The moment they do so, Krishna will follow after them and the Divine process of communication commences.

The awakening of Kaliya represents the initial stage of sadhana in which there develops an awareness of your own imperfection, an awareness of the impurities which lie within your personality. Of course, that awareness is not pleasant.

When Kaliya is awakened he tries to stifle Krishna. Similarly, when you begin your *sadhana* (spiritual discipline) and become aware of your impurities, you become restless, feeling that those egoistic imperfections are going to choke your spiritual aspiration. Krishna is the symbol of your spiritual aspiration. He has awakened Kaliya, he has uncovered the impurities that are hidden within the mind—but he remains unaffected by the venom of ego.

In your *sadhana*, as you continue to persist with *satsanga* and intensive self-effort, you realize that nothing can stifle your spiritual aspiration. No matter how many impurities you may have, no matter how many negative *samskaras* (impressions) from previous lives, nothing can stifle it. Once aspiration blossoms, it will continue to unfold more and more and it has miraculous power. Even though that Kaliya is a mighty dragon, it still will not succeed in stifling Krishna.

When *sadhana* moves into a state of concentration and meditation, the process of handling and overcoming the defects of your personality becomes easier. You develop the art of observing the negative *vrittis* or thought-waves of the mind and at the same time discover the spiritual strength to transform those negative *vrittis* into positive ones. Every negative *vritti*, when it is curbed, yields spiritual energy. In other words, anger is transformed into love, pride into humility, and greed into generosity. This is the subtle implication of the jewels released from the hoods of Kaliya as Krishna danced upon them. That divine dance of Krishna is symbolic of your ever-increasing spiritual strength.

Krishna's sending Kaliya away from the Yamuna River to abide in the ocean symbolizes the transition from ordinary egoistic awareness to the awareness that "I am all." As long as ego is in a conditioned mind, that ego produces egoism. But once your mind becomes unconditioned, once you develop ocean-like awareness, the ego in you becomes the universal "I Am"—*"Aham Asmi."* It is that transition from the ordinary awareness that "I Am the body" to the awareness that "I am That, I am the Self, I am all" that is implied by Krishna's sending Kaliya from Yamuna to abide in the ocean. The moment your ego moves away from the conditioned mind and establishes identity with the Absolute, your mind becomes absolutely purified and your heart becomes Vrindaban, where you can enjoy communion with God in the most delightful manner. There is nothing in the world as wonderful as being immersed in that atmosphere of Vrindaban, where Krishna plays His flute with eternal sweetness.

WITH this we conclude a brief study of the *shad-ripus*. May you not be harassed by these enemies of the soul, but handle them well, and make them tools for your evolution and ultimate victory.

As you pursue the process of integration day by day you will find that the serious evils of your past will drop away from you, like the old bark from trees. As the tree goes on growing, the old bark drops away, without surgery, without injuring the skin of the tree. Much in the same way, without much difficulty the negative will drop away from you. If you sincerely resolve to attain perfection even in this birth, you will be able to do it.

A person with a small flashlight in his hand may think, "This flashlight illumines only four yards of the road. How am I to go four miles with the help of this lamp?" That is foolish. Let him continue his march; and the flashlight will illumine the path ahead as he goes along.

Similarly, however feeble your will may seem at this moment, if you take recourse to good association, study elevating scriptures, practice selfless service, develop love of God, meditate and inquire, "Who am I?" you will move forward on the path of purifying your heart—and as you advance, the power of that Divine flashlight illumining your way will continue to increase more and more.

You are essentially a fountain of strength. Be positive. Vibrate with power and confidence. You have within you the cosmic source of all truth, beauty and auspiciousness. You are not this mortal personality. You are the immortal Self, the epitome of Perfection!

II

INSIGHT INTO DIVINE FEELING

(BHAVANA)

WHAT IS BHAVANA?

Bhavana is the most important factor leading to spiritual evolution. In fact, *bhavana* is the source of all that is good and beautiful in society, culture, and all relationships.

The Sanskrit term, itself, implies feeling blended with attitude, a quality of the heart. If you possess positive *bhavana*, a feeling that is positive and sublime, you move on the spiritual path with rapid strides. But if you possess negative *bhavana* or a degrading feeling, your movement is impeded.

Bhavana is also the secret behind the formation of karmas. What you do externally in itself does not carry much value; but the attitude with which you perform an action gives value to that action. You may do many things, but if you do not approach your actions with a selfless, Yogic attitude, you create many karmic entanglements. On the other hand, when you have a proper attitude and feeling, even though you may be doing little things, you are bringing about a great change in yourself.

There is an interesting story about a *sanyasi* (renunciate) who resided in a big building in the city. Across the street was another building inhabited by worldly people with one particular room taken by a prostitute. Although he didn't want to look in that direction, each time the *sanyasi* got up in the morning, his mind led him to do so. Whenever he saw anyone going into her room, his mind became agitated with feelings of remorse for their lost and fallen souls. Thus, his day was filled with distraction and frustration. Neither could he move away nor could he ask her to move away.

Though the lady had been a prostitute to begin with, she was now changing her lifestyle and aspiring to be better. Each time she looked towards the *sanyasi's* window, she thought how fortunate she was to be able to have his *darshan* (the sight of a holy man). And when people came to her apartment, she tried to impress the need of spirituality upon them.

As time passed, both the *sanyasi* and the lady aged and, curiously enough, both died on the same day. At the time of death, the *Yama dutas* (the messengers of *Yama*, the god of death) caught hold of the soul of this *sanyasi* and carried him to Yama's realm, where it would be decided whether he would go to heaven or hell. The *sanyasi* naturally was expecting to be given the highest level of heaven, but, to his great surprise, he was sentenced to the lowest level.

While reflecting upon his predicament, he saw the soul of the street-lady pass by, clad in shining robes and wonderful heavenly flowers. All around her, celestial beings were honoring her and a celestial chariot awaited to take her to the high planes. He asked the *Yama dutas*, "Aren't you making a mistake? A person such as that street-lady should be rotting in hell!" A *Yama duta* stepped forward. "Well, since you knew her on earth, why don't you ask her yourself?"

So the *sanyasi* approached the lady, effulgent in her astral body. She was delighted to see him and said, "I am so thankful to you. Because of you, I will ascend to the higher worlds." The *sanyasi* stood silent in amazement. "Each time I saw you, my mind rejoiced that God had placed me in the presence of such a wonderful holy man. The reason for your downfall is that when you looked at me, your mind moved towards worldly and negative thoughts. Thus, you went on generating negative impressions. I, on the other hand, was generating positive impressions due to my *bhavana.*"

Bhavana is the feeling arising from your unconscious impressions. If negative impressions dominate your unconscious, your feeling will be cramped.

A mind dominated by negative impressions always sees the negative in others and tends to judge others in a gross and negative manner. On the other hand, when you promote feelings of goodwill and magnanimity, you generate positive impressions in your unconscious mind, which, in turn, change your entire personality for the better. This is the case even in people who seem to be crude in nature. If they exhibit just the slightest Divine spark and that spark is encouraged, they will change for the better.

As you advance on the spiritual path, you learn how to develop and promote these positive feelings through *satsanga* (good association), study of scriptures, practice of meditation, and selfless service. All these enable you to change your personality and allow your mind to draw positive impressions. They must be practised with great diligence and perseverance, however.

Also understand that *bhavana* is not imagination, although imagination is slightly involved. When you promote positive *bhavana*, for example, you develop the feeling that God is in everyone and every object. In practical life, however, that *bhavana* should not interfere with your day to day realities.

For example, though you can worship God in fire, it does not mean you can stick your hand in it. Similarly, while you develop the feeling that God is in everyone, in normal life, you should be practical. Do not, in the name of *bhavana*, open your doors at night and invite the whole world in or place your jewelry out in the yard, hanging it on the trees for the picking. That is not the teaching. The development of *bhavana* is an internal development. Although it changes your personality, it does not affect your practical realities.

Great emphasis is given in Yoga on developing *bhavana*. *Bhavana* is your treasure. What matters is not the world in which you live, but the way you look at it, your attitude. Every action you perform with a higher feeling, therefore, takes on great merit and becomes a potent force in purifying the mind.

Impure and Pure Bhavana

Bhavana is of two types, according to which of the three *gunas* (modes of nature) predominates: *sattwa* (purity or harmony), *rajas* (restlessness or externalization) and *tamas* (inertia or dullness). *Rajasic* and *tamasic bhavana* are of a negative nature and come under the category of *ashubha bhavana* (impure feeling). For example, if you feel delighted because someone gets in trouble, that type of feeling in your heart is *rajasic* or *tamasic*. If your happiness depends upon proving your greatness before others by putting them down, that type of feeling is also *ashubha* (impure).

Rajasic bhavana is based on desire, anger, greed, jealousy, pride, and other impurities in their mild state. *Tamasic bhavana* develops when these impurities become intense, assuming the form of revenge, violent wrath, intense passion, inordinate greed, and the like.

Contrarily, *shubha* or *satwic bhavana* (pure feeling) is based on humility, goodness of the heart, contentment, devotion to God, and sublime experiences of meditation and *samadhi.* In order to advance on the path to Self-realization, then, you should promote *shubha bhavana* and eradicate *ashubha bhavana.*

Shubha or *satwic bhavana* is the most precious treasure for any individual. There is immediate joyousness the moment such *bhavana* surges in your heart. Negative *bhavana*, on the other hand, contracts the heart and brings about a feeling of internal suffocation. Due to mental perversion, however, one enjoys such a feeling. After people have become addicted to smoking, they actually enjoy it, even though the beginning of the habit brought nothing but choking and suffocation.

People who enjoy hurting others, due to their impure *bhavana*, bring about contraction in their own hearts, and become degraded in their own eyes. On the other hand, a feeling of understanding, profound love, willingness to serve others, and a feeling that God dwells in all is a most magnanimous feeling, and elevates one who promotes it.

However, developing *satwic bhavana* is not an easy task. You need to be persevering, forgiving, patient and enduring. A simple illustration is given about a saint who went to take a bath in a lake. As he entered the lake, he saw a scorpion and held out his hand to help it climb out of the lake. But instead of climbing onto the saint's hand, the frantic scorpion stung it. Naturally it was quite painful, but controlling himself, the saint again put his hand forward. Again the scorpion stung him.

Someone watching from the bank said, "O Saint, why don't you just let that stupid scorpion drown? Why let yourself be stung like that?" The saint answered, "If that scorpion does not give up his nature, stupid as he is, why should I give up mine? He clings to his; I must cling to mine." Ultimately, he saved the scorpion and rejoiced in accomplishing that task.

The story tells us that hatred is not the answer when dealing with those who are inimical and constantly stepping on your toes. Most people think that the moment someone gets in their way, the simplest solution is to develop ill will towards him. But that is not the right solution. Even though it may seem easy and justifiable to develop a sense of animosity towards such a person and, on that basis, harm him or delight in seeing him crushed, such behavior is degrading from a spiritual point of view because it maintains impressions of hatred in your heart. When hatred overpowers your personality, you have actually failed as a human being.

In the Divine Plan, such failure is not allowed. You will need to be born again in order to learn to love the person you hated in this life. In the Divine Plan, relationships are adjusted in a strange manner. You have to learn that the person you hated so much can also be loved. So, if you want to avoid that long-range learning process of coming back again and again, you must start practising a higher type of feeling.

Goodwill must, therefore, be promoted towards people who are crude, inimical and who, like the scorpion, repeatedly hurt others. Let them do what they want. You must develop an understanding that God abides in all.

It is due to your own karmas that certain people become responsible for causing agitation in your personality. The idea that these negative people are the cause of your unhappiness is not true. These people have been appointed by Divine Will, according to your karma, to make you struggle a little, so that you can find resistance in your life and thereby evolve. Realize, then, that behind the mask of negative people, there is a Divine Hand. A saintly figure lies in even the most crude and wicked personality; everyone is a potential saint or sage. By promoting the revelation of that saintliness in others, your own feeling finds great fulfillment.

There are numerous illustrations of this. You may struggle through a certain relationship for years, enduring much suffering and sacrifice. Finally, the person who has been the cause of so much pain and misery realizes his error and develops a genuine repentance. When you see the tears of remorse flowing from the eyes of those who have been so crude and cruel, a Divine feeling surges in your heart, and you realize you have truly succeeded.

It is different, however, when you compel a person to be subservient, thwart him by causing fear, or threaten him into acting according to your expectations. Anyone can be good when you have a rod in your hand. Even a ferocious lion acts like a kitten under a big whip. If this is your method of influencing others, then the feeling in your heart is a fearful one. What would happen if you didn't have that whip? Behind those who assert their dominance with power or force lies a fearful and contracted heart.

But when you develop a gentle and saintly nature, and thereby see people change because of your endurance and sacrifice, the problem is resolved forever and the force of spirituality and love triumphs. But when the force of pride or ego wins, the problem is not resolved, but rather follows you from life to life.

From Bhavana to Bhav

Feeling becomes like a stagnant river when it is overpowered by *rajas* and *tamas*—by hatred, greed, restless desires of the mind, selfishness. This state is degrading for the soul. You may possess great estates surrounded by wondrous gardens resplendent with numerous flowers, but if the flowers of Divine virtues do not bloom in your heart, if your heart has become a field containing negative feelings, then all your external attainments become insignificant. An aspirant must, therefore, employ great vigilance in cultivating a higher form of feeling that is free of ego and dominated by *sattwa* (purity).

As *sattwic bhavana* (feeling based on compassion, selflessness, and goodness of the heart) is developed, it gradually becomes concentrated into what is known as *bhav* (Divine feeling). It is this Divine feeling that is offered to God and links you with Him. Both *bhavana* and *bhav* are feeling; however, one is diffused like humidity in the atmosphere, and the other is concentrated like a cloud. The difference is very similar to that between *dharana* (concentration) and *dhyana* (meditation) in Raja Yoga. In *dharana*, the mind is being focused; in *dhyana*, the focused state continues. In the same manner, in the state of *bhavana*, feeling is being focused and withdrawn from the outer world and directed towards God. In the state of *bhav*, the intensified feeling flows spontaneously.

From the Shallow to the Sublime

On the path to God, *bhav* is the great secret. Ordinary feeling cannot capture God. When people read books of devotion, their normal sentiments are aroused. They pray with a melting heart, shed tears, plead and, after a while, when their prayers are not answered, they wipe their tears and feel that their prayers have been wasted. But *bhav* is of a different nature. It arises in one who has a genuine feeling that God is All, the Soul of the soul, the object of supreme love. This type of sincere awareness develops in a personality that is highly integrated and free of ego.

The vast majority of people experience the impact of worldly feeling—feeling guided by passion, worldly love, or infatuation. Under the impact of that feeling, physical changes occur in the body: the voice chokes, tears flow from the eyes, palpitations occur, there is a sense of thrill all over the body. Most people experience these symptoms under the influence of shallow feeling.

Similar sensations occur as one follows the spiritual path and develops *satwic* feeling that gradually becomes concentrated into *bhav*. However, these sensations brought about by deep devotion have a totally different direction and quality than those similar expressions of love produced by shallow, worldly feeling.

In a devotee who has developed *bhav*, just hearing the name of God or thinking about a saintly person brings about a sense of thrill. The story of Lord Jesus, Krishna, Rama, or any saint causes the heart to melt as feeling is drawn by a Divine magnet toward God.

Ramakrishna Paramahamsa was famous for shedding tears. Whenever he sang the Divine name or even thought of God, tears flowed from his eyes. That is one expression of *satwic bhav*. There is such joy, such a rare and unique experience within, that tears flow. But those tears are not tears of spiritual sadness, they are tears of spiritual bliss. It is said that there are two types of tears — hot and cold. When one has bitterness, sorrow, or grief, the tears are hot.

When one has an upsurge of Divine sentiment, the tears are cooling and refreshing to the eyes.

There are many other such physical manifestations of this development. There is an eagerness in the eyes, a change in the color of the face as the impact of Divine feeling is felt. When Moses stood before the luminous fire in the presence of God, there was a luminosity in his face and people were bewildered. When *satwic* feeling develops, a subtle aura envelops the personality and many changes occur in one's behavior.

An aspirant must discipline himself through *satsanga* (good association) and Karma Yoga (selfless service of humanity) and embark on a rigorous overhauling of personality in order to allow the heart to capture Divine feeling, *bhav*. As he does so, the expressions of shallow sentiments in his personality will be replaced by expressions of profound feeling that reflect the deep transformation of his inner life.

THE FIVE DEVOTIONAL ATTITUDES

Bhav is attained through any of the five devotional attitudes given in Bhakti Yoga: *shanta* (peaceful); *dasya* (master-servant); *sakhya* (friend-friend); *vatsalya* (parent-child); *madhurya* (lover-beloved). Develop any one of these attitudes towards God and you will experience unparalled bliss. That special feeling that gathers in your heart is *bhav*, and the joy experienced is known as *rasa* (nectarine delight).

Shanta Bhav

The first attitude, *shanta* (peaceful) *bhav*, is characterized by a secret love of God which is not expressed externally. The classic example of one who adopted this type of devotion is Bhishma in the *Mahabharata*. Bhishma always loved Krishna but in a hidden, non-expressive way. Bhishma was duty-bound to fight for the Kauravas and therefore, during the Mahabharata battle he was actually fighting against Krishna and Arjuna. Though fighting externally, internally he considered it Divine play. In truth, his mind and heart were devoted to Krishna. On one occasion, when the fight was intense, Krishna realized that Arjuna was wavering in the performance of his duty because he was considering Bhishma as his grandfather. That attitude was obstructing his performance as a warrior. So, in order to teach him a lesson, Krishna jumped out of His chariot with a wheel in His hand, ready to strike Bhishma. Bhishma began to pray to Krishna, not out of fear, but out of joy that Krishna Himself had come to fight against him.

Dasya Bhav

The second devotional attitude is *dasya bhav.* "I am a slave and God is the Master." Through the perfection of this attitude one experiences *dasya rasa*, the special nectarine sweetness of Divine love. The term "slave" generally has a negative connotation, but in the mystical world, being a slave to God is the loftiest development. If you are truly a slave to God, you are a saint. You have no ego of your own. You become merely an instrument in Divine Hands. The classic illustration of *dasya bhav* is the profound love of Hanuman for Rama, a love that gave rise to the most inspired, selfless, heroic and sublime acts of devotion.

Another illustration of *dasya bhav* is contained in the Sufi tale of the slave, Luqman, and his rich master. The master loved Luqman because he was so obedient and good-hearted. In fact, inwardly he adored his slave and admired his wonderful qualities. Outwardly, he acted as a master. One day, the rich man called Luqman to sit with him and share one of the melons he had been given as a gift. He gave a slice of melon to his slave. As Luqman ate it, his eyes sparkled with joy. Seeing this, the master sliced another piece and gave it to him. Again the slave ate, showing his obvious delight in the exquisite taste of the fruit. And so it went, until the last slice, which the master decided to eat himself. He eagerly put it in his mouth only to find that it was so sour and bitter that he had to spit it out. Puzzled, he asked his slave, "Why did you not say it was bitter? Why didn't you spit it out? Why did you let me go on giving you that?" Luqman replied, "O Master, you have done so many good things for me. In the midst of the thousands of sweetnesses you have bestowed on me, this little sourness hardly matters. In truth, because your loving hand touched it, it was transformed and nothing was more delicious."

You should try to understand how many blessings God has given you, how much sweetness He has conferred upon you. Now and then He may give you a little problem, a little adversity, but there is always a Divine intention behind it. Out of infinite wisdom, God leads every soul through various conditions; what appears bitter is, in reality, sweet. What appears as a curse is actually a blessing in disguise. When you begin to understand this, there is no sense of contradiction, no turning away from God. Rather, there is delight that God, who has given so many good things, now and then gives out a slice of bitter melon—and really, since it has come from the Divine Hand, how can there be any bitterness?

So, with that overpowering spiritual feeling, you convert adversity into prosperity. The bitterness of adversity turns into the sweetness of Divine grace. If that vision is adopted, life becomes joyous. Your personality becomes relaxed. Ultimately, when you have shed your ego completely, your spirit becomes One with God. This is the essence of *dasya bhav*.

Sakya Bhav

In *sakhya bhav*, the heart of the devotee develops the feeling that God is not distant, that He can be befriended. A friendship is a very special type of relationship. With a friend you share your feelings, but you do not overburden him or her with your problems. You may become angry with your friend, but at the same time there is the feeling that the bonds of friendship can never be severed. If friendship is true, external differences do not matter.

In the same manner, you develop this type of feeling towards God: God is your friend and He is always there to confide in. There is also a concern not to burden Him too much with your problems. Also you can be certain that the deep bonds of friendship are everlasting, and that no amount of discord can ever sever them.

Furthermore, you know that God, being your friend, will come to your rescue. A simple illustration is given from the Sufi literature. A certain saint regularly performed miracles, and for this reason many people were suspicious of and antagonistic towards him.

Once a dead body was brought to this saint. When he invoked God's name, saying, "In the name of God may this man come back to life," the corpse didn't come to life. However, then the saint invoked his own name, saying, "In my name may he come to life," and the man came to life! This saint was so attuned to God that God glorified him in this way, to the consternation of the people around who thought the saint was blasphemous in assuming that he could be as glorious as God Himself.

In *Srimad Bhagavat Purana*, the story about Krishna and Sudama well illustrates the glory of friendliness towards God. Sudama and Krishna were classmates when they were young. But as time passed Krishna became a great emperor endowed with immense prosperity and glory, while Sudama remained a poor *brahmin*, too poor to even maintain himself and his wife.

One day his wife reminded him, "You have a great friend in Krishna, not an ordinary one. Why don't you go to Him. He will give you all that you need." Urging him to go, she gave him a present for Krishna—a small bag of fried rice. Sudhama, dressed in his ragged clothes, took that small bag and walked all the way to Dwaraka, where Krishna ruled. After many days of suffering and turmoil, he reached the palace, but the gatekeepers would not let him in. Sudama said, "Go and report to your master that I am His friend and have come to see Him." So one of the gatekeepers went and reported this to Krishna.

The moment Krishna heard this, He jumped up from His throne, shook off His crown and shed His royal robes, pushed away His attendants and rushed to meet the *brahmin*, embracing him with great affection. Then to the consternation of the queens, Krishna placed Sudama on the throne and Himself started washing Sudama's feet. Then Krishna asked whether the *brahmin's* wife had given some offering or some type of food. Sudama was ashamed to give that little bag of rice to Krishna, so he tried to hide it from Him. Krishna, realizing this, snatched the bag from his hands and started eating the fried rice. He ate one handful, two handfuls. Then the queens stopped Krishna from eating any more and they themselves had their share. That rice was supremely delightful to all.

Soon Sudama had to depart. Krishna had not given him anything at all, or so Sudama thought, but Sudama did not mind. He did not have any negative feelings towards Krishna. He only knew that he had been reunited with a wonderful friend. It was only upon his return home that Sudama realized a miracle had happened while he was gone. His little hut had been converted into a palace. The entire village itself had been converted into a heavenly land and all the people were like angels. His wife had been transformed into a great queen and all was wonderful. Krishna had indeed honored his friend.

In one sense, every individual is Sudama, and if you develop that type of devotion towards God, He will come running from His heavenly palace where He sits on eternity and is towered over by infinity. Shaking off that eternal state, He will come rushing towards you.

Being in this world, what you have to offer will seem like nothing more than that little bag of rice. However, whatever good karmas you have will be glorified because God accepts whatever you have done according to your capacity. You become His friend.

The moment you become God's friend, the internal structure of your unconscious is overhauled. While before it was an ordinary village with huts, now it becomes a kingly estate with palatial buildings. All *samskaras* (impressions) become Divine. The wife of Sudama symbolizes intellect, which becomes intuitive. And so, if you develop this attitude of friendliness towards God, you will be led to Divine Realization and the attainment of Supreme Glory. That is the glory of *sakhya bhav.*

Vatsalya Bhav | The fourth form of devotional feeling is known as *vatsalya bhav*, an attitude compared to a mother's love for her child. You begin to feel that God is like a child. A mother does not expect anything in return for her love, but rather feels fulfilled simply by loving the child. So too, a devotee who has advanced begins to enjoy the sweetness of Divine love to such an extent that he does not expect anything in return. As long as you are expecting something in return, your devotion remains limited, restricted. But when you enter that advanced state, the very fact of merely remembering God fills your heart with great joy.

For one whose devotion is not mature, prayer is often a means to an end. You pray, and then wait for the results. When those results do not come, you feel frustrated. But, as you advance, by the very act of praying you are opening your heart to God and not to the world outside with its perishable objects. Prayer, in itself, brings about an awakening of great joy.

A parable is told of a devotee who goes to a temple and prays and prays, and then becomes frustrated when his prayers go seemingly unanswered. He says, "I have been praying to God but there has been no response. Is God deaf?" God, assuming the form of a person who happens to be close by, says, "The very fact that you have been praying is the answer to your prayer. It is God's grace that has allowed you to open your heart to God. The very fact that you are praying is a Divine pull drawing your soul away from the world." So, as you advance, you do not expect anything in return for your acts of love. This is an attitude Hindu mystics compare to the love of parents for their child.

Stories are given in the *Puranas* of how Lord Krishna, God-incarnate, was loved by his mother, Yashoda. Yashoda was a highly advanced personality. In her previous life she had practised great austerity, and she had held the desire that God should incarnate as her child. So she had the great joy of being associated with Krishna. Krishna as a child was not an ordinary child. All those who came into contact with Krishna, even while he was just three or four years old, were thrilled at the very sight of him.

The *gopis*, cowherd women who sold various milk products, were so delighted to see Krishna that on any pretext they would come to his house just to look at him. Krishna, in turn, went into their houses and did the naughty things that children do. For example, he would enter stealthily into a house and break jars of butter or yogurt. Pretending to be angry, but really just wanting a pretext to see Krishna,

the *gopis* would go to Yashoda's house and complain, "Where is your son? That master of thieves has been breaking the jars and eating the newly churned butter!"

One day Yashoda became terribly angry. However, there was sweetness in that anger. She said playfully, "I am going to teach him a good lesson." She went after Krishna and he ran away from her as if he were frightened. Finally she caught hold of him and tried to tie him up. But every rope she found fell short because Krishna would swell himself up. Finally, after she had tried many times, she became exhausted. Krishna, knowing that she was exhausted, then allowed himself to be tied up.

Yashoda tied him to a wooden structure that was used for husking rice. It was a strong, heavy structure, one a child could not move. Krishna stayed tied up, tears trickling down his cheeks. Seeing this, the *gopis* said, "Mother Yashoda, please let him go." But this time she was firm. She said, "I will not let him go. You were the cause. You were always complaining about him." So Krishna stayed tied up while his mother engaged herself in her work.

When he saw that no one was around, Krishna pushed the whole big structure and it started rolling behind him towards the house. In front of the house were two Arjuna trees. They were gigantic twin trees in the form of a fork. Krishna wedged that structure between the two trees in such a way that with a heavy pull he uprooted both of them, and they came crashing down. Everyone came running. His mother took him in her arms and was joyous that he was unharmed.

The mystic implication of this story is that, in devotional movement, you collect all the strings of your heart, all the feelings, and integrate them in order to capture God within your heart. In this process, the purity of feeling, compassion, and goodness that you develop is like butter. Tying Krishna up is symbolic of integrating your feelings. After integrating your feelings, there still has to be surrender to God. When Krishna is tied up in your heart, he uproots attachment and hatred *(raga and dwesha)*, those two gigantic trees that have roots in your ego. Devotion effaces your ego and, thereby, uproots attachment and hatred.

Mother Yashoda's love for Krishna exemplifies *vatsalya bhav*, and there are many saints in India who have adopted that attitude. When you adopt the attitude that God is like a child and you bestow all your love upon Him without any expectation of something in return, that is an advanced level of devotion. When you pray for the sake of prayer, love for the sake of loving, God becomes a mass of tenderness and sweetness. Such is the glory of *vatsalya bhav*.

Madhurya Bhav

As you advance in Divine Love, you gradually notice the disappearance of your own individuality, your own desires. In the beginning, you develop love of God as a means to an end. You worship God with the expectation of a response. As you advance, that expectation diminishes. It does not matter whether Divinity responds or not. The very experience of Divine Love becomes the source of boundless joy.

One of the sweetest states of *bhav* is known as *madhurya bhav*, literally meaning "sweet sentiment." It is described in worldly terms as that feeling that exists between lover and beloved.

Mystics have written many poems and verses describing this state. Those who are not initiated into the path of devotion are easily misled by these songs of love. Although the language used to express this type of love is that used by the masses, this loving feeling has nothing to do with the erotic form of love, love based on passion. Why, then is this language used? Because there is no other way to express *madhurya bhav* to the masses. Sages describe the lofty state of superconsciousness known as *samadhi* by comparing it to sleep, yet sleep is far away from *samadhi*. Similarly, the Divine union, the profound feeling of love towards God, is described in worldly terms as the feeling of love between lover and beloved in order to help aspirants understand that transcendental state in which self-awareness is lost.

This type of writing has been prevalent since ancient times. In the Bible there are passages in Solomon's songs that seem to be the words of a lover describing the beloved. However, they are designed to show the mutual relationship between God and the soul, the state in which Divine love devours the individuality of a person. This is the most advanced state—a state in which ego ceases to exist.

A parable is told to explain that point. Once Sage Narada wanted to know who were the best devotees of Lord Krishna. Krishna proposed a simple method for determining this. He was going to pretend that he had a stomach ache and, further, that it would be cured only when a devotee offered him water to drink in which the devotee's foot had been dipped. Krishna was going to pretend that if any devotee were to give him that type of water, his pain would be cured. Narada eagerly agreed to that plan. He went to some famous devotees and asked, "Will you help Lord Krishna? He is suffering from a stomach ache and only a devotee can come to his aid."

One devotee said, "I will do anything for the Lord." Narada then said, "Here is a jar of water. Put your foot into it. Krishna is going to drink from this and that will cure him, because a devotee is always greater that God." But the devotee said, "How could I ever allow Krishna to drink something in which my foot has been dipped? What will happen to me?" Narada replied, "Surely you will go to hell for having done so." The devotee said, "Well then, I will not do this."

One by one the devotees said the same thing. No one would allow his foot to be dipped into water for Krishna to drink. Then Narada came to Radha, the famous devotee who had developed *madhurya bhav*, the state of intense sweetness towards Krishna. Narada said, "Krishna is suffering from stomach pain." And Radha said, "What should I do to help?" He said, "All you have to do is to put your foot into this water and Krishna will drink it." Radha's feet were besmeared with mud, but she was immediately willing to put them into that water. Narada said, "Stop, think it over before you do this. If you allow this water to be taken by Krishna you are going to everlasting hell." Radha answered, "Who cares about hell? My beloved is suffering from pain and all you can talk about is hell! What type of Saint are you? Bring all of that water." And she placed both her feet into the water.

Narada realized that here was the greatest devotee of all. Radha's love was not conditioned by her egoistic expectations. Even if she had to enter hell in order to please the Lord, she was ready to do so. There was no consideration for her own ego. That is the characteristic of *madhurya bhav*. When your devotional sentiment has reached its height, ego does not matter at all. Whether you are placed in an adverse situation or a prosperous one, love for God will not diminish. It will continue to grow even if you are repeatedly given adversity.

As a beginner on the spiritual path, you may pray and meditate today, and tomorrow you may find that your day is even more miserable than today. Or you may practise some Yoga and then find your condition does not improve the way you expected, but rather becomes more complicated. If these things happen, you may become discouraged and say, "What is the point of practising Yoga or worshipping God if my conditions do not improve?" But the fact is, as you advance, you realize there is the constant possibility of loving God no matter what happens. That love cannot be interrupted. Whether there is adversity or prosperity, Divine love never diminishes.

If you were to develop love for God, how joyous, how engrossing that would be! If you were to have the slightest glimpse or experience of that love, then your life would flow towards God no matter what

your conditions, whether there was prosperity or adversity. As you advance, you will realize that the intellect of a devotee does not interpret anything in the world as adversity. Rather, it finds every condition to be a Divine gift.

Sometimes there are painful situations, yet they have a profound mystical meaning for your soul. When you become aware of that meaning, you realize that those painful situations are not really painful, but that you are being led to higher wisdom by God, Who is the embodiment of supreme love.

In the state of *madhurya bhav*, one experiences intense sweetness towards the Divine Self. Ego melts and the devotee becomes one with God.

Devotees generally choose one of the five devotional attitudes or states of *bhav* that suits them best, and while other attitudes are practised, their chosen attitude becomes predominant. Through any one of the five attitudes, one can attain perfection and enjoy the greatest heights of Divine communion.

For Tulsidas, the author of the *Ramayana*, the predominant attitude was *dasya bhav* ("God is the master and I am the slave.") For Surdas, another great devotee, the attitude was *vatsalya bhav* ("God is like a child, I am a parent"). It is said that once these two saints were walking along the road, talking together, when a mad elephant came towards them. Tulsidas stayed on the road, while Surdas ran away into a ditch.

When asked why he had run away if he was a devotee of God, Surdas said, "Well, my God is a child. It is to protect Him that I ran away." Tulsidas, on the other hand, stood there in the road, relying on Rama—the master—and Rama mysteriously helped him out. This shows the uniqueness of attitude held by two great sages.

Saints may adopt a particular attitude or *bhav*, even though internally they have transcended all attitudes and have become one with God. They do so to teach these attitudes to aspirants. Though adopting a certain type of attitude, internally they have gone beyond all.

Maha Bhav | As feeling unfolds, a devotee ascends the different rungs leading to Divine communion—that state in which feeling is no longer limited by the ego, nor confined within your conditioned mind. When feeling becomes free, when it is touched with the light of intuition, that state is known as *maha bhav*. In that state a sage is perpetually in great ecstasy. It is a thrilling state of Divine communion, and the goal one must endeavor to realize.

Consider your heart like a room on a mountain cliff. It has been shut on all sides for a long time with ego keeping the air-conditioning on constantly. Now there comes a time when the gusty wind breaks open all the windows and the room is in communion with nature. There is no more restriction of the atmosphere. In the same manner, the human heart has been conditioned by egoistic feeling, attachments, and illusions; but by the progressive awakening of Divine love, the windows of your heart are flung open. Divine grace comes rushing in like a gusty wind and your soul is led to communion with the Divine Self. It is transported to the Divine realm. That state is known as *maha bhav,* Divine ecstasy.

Maha bhav is experienced by sages and saints perpetually in their internal life. Some sages express this externally, some do not. But those who are advanced and spiritually sensitive are able to understand the internal state of saints and sages. Ramakrishna Paramahamsa always shed tears and passed into ecstasy when listening to Divine praise or *kirtan.* Ramana Maharshi was always calm and cool. External expressions are varied, but the internal realization is the same.

In the state of *maha bhav,* everything becomes a mirror reflecting eternity. Every name and form becomes a transparent veil and, therefore, does not obstruct the vision of what underlies the names and forms: the Divine Self. Saints and sages who are enlightened experience God behind every name and form. All objects remind them of Divinity.

In a lesser level of devotion, there are majestic objects that give the message of God more effectively, more easily than ordinary objects. In the beginning, you remember God when you see glorious events like the sunrise and sunset. But as you advance, a brick wall, a tiny blade of grass, a little worm crawling, or even a piece of garbage brings an awareness of the Divine Presence behind it. That is the advanced state of *maha bhav*.

There is an episode in *Srimad Bhagavata* that illustrates the sublime nature of *maha bhav*. When Krishna left the *gopis* or cowherd maidens, never to return, Uddhava, Krishna's great friend, said, "Oh Krishna, I feel great sympathy for the *gopis* who were your devotees. Now they must be suffering intense separation from you." Krishna answered, "O friend, you are speaking what is right. I am sending you as a messenger, as my representative. Go and console those *gopis*."

Uddhava traveled to where the *gopis* lived in Vrindaban, and when he arrived all the *gopis* surrounded him and were delighted to see him. Then, in an attempt at consolation, he said, "Oh *gopis*, you must know that Krishna remembers you, and Krishna is not anyone's possession. He is the Divine Being." Radha, the most prominent *gopi*, smiled and said, "I am really surprised by what you are saying. You are saying that Krishna is not here in our midst? Krishna is much more in our midst now than ever. Are you dreaming? We hear the flute of Krishna, we see him taking the cows into the fields, we find him in the clouds and in the peacocks as they dance, we find him with us all the time."

Uddhava then humbly realized that his mystic experience was mediocre in comparison to the *gopis*, whose awareness of the Divine Presence was constant. In the beginning Krishna had been an external personality, but as devotion advanced He was no longer a human personality. He became the subtle essence behind everything. People who did not have that insight thought the *gopis* were miserable because Krishna had left them. But it was not really so. The physical Krishna disappeared from their midst but the spiritual Krishna permeated them and they were always in the state of awareness of Divine Presence. That is the state of *maha bhav*.

One who has attained that state is the highest evolved personality. On the tree of spiritual evolution, he is the highest blossom. The scriptures say that the whole world rejoices when a person attains that state. Gods rejoice in the heavenly world. The forefathers of such a person rejoice because they feel the pride of being related to that type of personality. To have a saint in one's family is considered one of the greatest achievements. According to Hindu thought, that saintly personality, figuratively speaking, purifies seven generations before and seven generations after.

The attainment of *maha bhav*, of Self-realization, occurs at a certain time in the depths of one's heart, in silence, in stillness. But it resounds like thunder through the cosmos. There is an immediate message that reverberates all over the universe. Such is the majesty of that state of greatest glory, the fulfillment of all human potential, the culmination of all love.

Author Swami Jyotirmayananda

About Swami Jyotirmayananda And His Ashram

Swami Jyotirmayananda was born on February 3, 1931, in a pious family in Dumari Buzurg, District Saran, Bihar, India—a northern province sanctified by the great Lord Buddha. From his early childhood he showed various marks of future saintliness. He was calm and reflective, compassionate to all, and a constant source of inspiration to all who came in contact with him. Side by side with his studies and practical duties, he reflected upon life's deeper purpose.

An overwhelming feeling to serve humanity through a spiritual life led him to embrace the ancient order of Sanyasa on February 3, 1953, at the age of 22. Living in the Himalayan retreats by the sacred River Ganges, he practised intense austerities. In tireless service of his Guru, Sri Swami Sivananda Maharaj, Swamiji taught at the Yoga Vedanta Forest Academy as a professor of religion. In addition to giving lectures on the Upanishads, Raja Yoga and all the important scriptures of India, he was the editor of the *Yoga Vedanta Journal.* Ever able to assist foreign students in their understanding of Yoga and Vedanta, his intuitive perception of their problems endeared him to all.

Swamiji's exemplary life, love towards all beings, great command of spiritual knowledge, and dynamic expositions on Yoga and Vedanta philosophy attracted enormous interest all over India. He frequently lectured by invitation at the All India Vedanta Conferences in Delhi, Amritsar, Ludhiana, and in other parts of India.

In 1962, after many requests, Swami Jyotirmayananda came to the West to spread the knowledge of India. As founder of Sanatan Dharma Mandir in Puerto Rico (1962-1969), Swamiji rendered unique service to humanity through his regular classes, weekly radio lectures in English and in Spanish, and numerous TV appearances.

In March, 1969, Swamiji moved to Miami, Florida, and established the ashram that has become the center for the international activities of the Yoga Research Foundation. Branches of this organization now exist throughout the world and spread the teachings of yoga to aspirants everywhere. In 1985, Swamiji founded an ashram near New Delhi, India, which is now serving the community by offering yoga classes, by publishing the Hindi Journal, *Yoganjali,* by assisting the needy through a medical clinic, and by furthering the education of children through the Bal Divya Jyoti Public School.

Today Swami Jyotirmayananda occupies a place of the highest order among the international men of wisdom. He is well-recognized as the foremost proponent of Integral Yoga, a way of life and thought that synthesizes the various aspects of the ancient yoga tradition into a comprehensive plan of personality integration.

Through insightful lectures that bring inspiration to thousands who attend the conferences, camps and philosophical gatherings, Swamiji shares the range and richness of his knowledge of the great scriptures of the world.

His monthly magazine—*International Yoga Guide*—is enjoyed by spiritual seekers throughout the world. His numerous books and cassette tapes are enriching the lives of countless aspirants who have longed for spiritual guidance that makes the most profound secrets of yoga available to them in a manner that is joyous and practical.

Despite the international scope of his activities, Swamiji still maintains an intimate setting at his main ashram in Miami that allows fortunate aspirants to have the privilege of actually studying and working under his direct guidance. In the lecture hall of the Foundation, Swami Jyotirmayananda personally conducts an intense weekly schedule of classes in *Bhagavad Gita, Yoga Vasistha, Mahabharata, Upanishads, Panchadashi*, the *Bible*, Raja Yoga, Hatha Yoga and meditation.

With a work/study scholarship, qualified students are able to attend all classes conducted by Swamiji tuition-free. In return, students devote their energy and talents to the Foundation's noble mission by serving in the bookshop, offices, press, and computer and publication facilities.

Both the Yoga Research Foundation and the main ashram lie in the southwest section of Miami, two minutes from the University of Miami and 15 minutes from the Miami International Airport. The main ashram is on a two and a half acre plot surrounded by trees and exotic plants, reminiscent of the forest hermitages of the ancient sages. Adjoining are subsidiary ashrams that house student residents and Foundation guests. The grounds are picturesque, abounding with tall eucalyptus and oak trees, a fragrant mango orchard giving shelter to numerous birds and squirrels, and a lake of lotus blooms reflecting the expansion of the sky. In this serene yet dynamic environment, the holy presence of Swami Jyotirmayananda fills the atmosphere with the silent, powerful message of Truth, and the soul is nurtured and nourished, allowing for a total education and evolution of one's inner Self.

BOOKS

by Swami Jyotirmayananda

From ancient times, the devotional beauty of the epic story of Rama has given untold inspiration and delight to countless aspirants. In *Mysticism of the Ramayana,* the subtle philosophical implications of this colorful epic are illumined by Sri Swami Jyotirmayananda's spiritual insight, and the infinite grandeur of the Ramayana truly shines forth. In the gracious light of Swamiji's vision, all spiritual seekers will soar on the wings of devotion and wisdom to the highest summits of spiritual bliss!

MYSTICISM
OF THE
RAMAYANA

$11.95

Prices subject to change

Cassettes

45-minute/$10.00 each

881
Don't Look Back
The Philosophy of Desires

882
The Philosophy of Expectations
Prayer

883
Insight into Knowledge
Always be Thoughtful

884
How to Conserve Mental Energy
Insight into Good Manners

885
How to Overcome Insecurity
Insight into Sadhana (Spiritual Discipline)

886
Insight into Abhyasa (Repeated Effort)
Insight into Vairagya (Dispassion)

887
How to Handle Grief
How to Overcome Demoniac Qualities

888
Insight into Bliss
The Philosophy of Time

889
Insight into Bhavana (Devotional Feeling)
How to Overcome Hatred

890
How to Overcome the Sense of Insecurity
The Virtue of Patience

891
How to Overcome Prejudice
Insight into Selfless Action

892
Insight into Worship
Insight into Prosperity

893
A Message for Students
Insight into Death

894
How to Overcome Mental Distraction
Insight into Dharma

895
Insight into Compassion
Insight into Faith

896
Insight into Foresight
How to Develop Fortitude

897
Develop Purity of Intellect
The Philosophy of War

898
The Evils of Revenge
Insight into Egoism

899
Mysticism of Shivaratri
Overcoming Intolerance

900
Insight into Liberation
The Virtue of Patience

901
Insight into Renunciation
The Philosophy of Idol Worship

902
The Virtue of Fortitude
Imagination

903
Fate and Free Will
The Quest for Peace

904
Insight into Death
Insight into Miracles

905
How to Face Adversity
Insight into Detachment

906
Purity of Intellect
Tenacity

907
Insight into Nonduality
Insight into Dharma (Righteousness)

908
Insight into Meditation I
Insight into Meditation II

909
Insight into Dreams
Insight into Peace

910
Insight into Mental Strength
Insight into Miracles

911
How to Overcome Mean-Mindedness
Insight into Japa Yoga

912
Insight into Karma Yoga
Insight into Jnana Yoga

913
Insight into Freedom
How to Overcome Pessimism

914
Insight into Integral Yoga
Glory of Satsanga

915
Four Types of Devotees
How to Come Closer to God

916
How to Develop Fortitude
Insight into Desire

Many more titles available !